T0270877

Building Urban Resilience

This is one of the first few books to discuss the Covid-19 crisis as an urban phenomenon and illustrates this through the case of Singapore and its pandemic response efforts.

The book describes the implications and impacts of the pandemic on Singapore's urban landscape, economy, and society. It also assesses the urban interventions that have emerged in response to the pandemic. It examines the spatial implications and challenges of delineating safe distancing in various public and commercial spaces and evaluates the effectiveness of these interventions. The book also explains how Singapore's smart city capabilities help with its Covid-19 response.

This book will be of great interest to urban planners, healthcare professionals, and policymakers across the world, particularly those who are hoping to learn from the success and limitations of Singapore's Covid-19 responses.

J.J. Woo is Senior Lecturer at the Lee Kuan Yew School of Public Policy, National University of Singapore. He has previously held faculty and research positions at the Education University of Hong Kong, Nanyang Technological University, and the John F. Kennedy School of Government, Harvard University. His research focuses on policy design, urban governance, and crisis management, with a strong focus on global cities in Asia. Dr Woo is the author of several books on economic policy and crisis response in Asia. His research has also been published in leading international peer-reviewed journals.

Debbie R. Loo is an architect by training with a background in professional practice, urban studies research, and teaching. She has worked on numerous built projects in Singapore, most notably Pinnacle @ Duxton, an international award-winning public residential project. She has held research roles in urban studies think-tanks, such as the Lee Kuan Yew Centre for Innovative Cities and SUTD-MIT International Design Centre. Her research interests include ageing urbanism, urban policy, and heritage conservation.

Routledge Research in Sustainable Planning and Development in Asia
Series Editor: Richard Hu

Urban Flood Risk Management
Looking at Jakarta
Christopher Silver

Data-centric Regenerative Built Environment
Big Data for Sustainable Regeneration
Saeed Banihashemi and Sepideh Zarepour Sohi

Disaster Resilience and Sustainability
Japan's Urban Development and Social Capital
Hitomi Nakanishi

Megaregional China
Richard Hu

Building Urban Resilience
Singapore's Policy Response to Covid-19
J.J. Woo and Debbie R. Loo

Urban Renewal in Central Seoul
Planning Paradigm Shifts
Hyung Min Kim

For more information about this series, please visit: www.routledge.com/Routledge-Research-in-Sustainable-Planning-and-Development-in-Asia/book-series/RRSPDA

Building Urban Resilience

Singapore's Policy Response
to Covid-19

J.J. Woo and Debbie R. Loo

Routledge
Taylor & Francis Group

LONDON AND NEW YORK

First published 2025
by Routledge
4 Park Square, Milton Park, Abingdon, Oxon OX14 4RN

and by Routledge
605 Third Avenue, New York, NY 10158

Routledge is an imprint of the Taylor & Francis Group, an informa business

© 2025 J.J. Woo and Debbie R. Loo

British Library Cataloguing in Publication Data
A catalogue record for this book is available from the British Library

ISBN: 978-0-367-69617-7 (hbk)
ISBN: 978-0-367-69619-1 (pbk)
ISBN: 978-1-003-14255-3 (ebk)

DOI: 10.4324/9781003142553

Typeset in Times New Roman
by Apex CoVantage, LLC

To our son, Harvey

Contents

Figures

Acknowledgements

We remember the early days of January 2020 in Hong Kong, where we lived and were preparing to leave for Singapore. It was the cusp of the first flurry of news reports about a certain virus circulating in the region – and no one was yet the wiser then. This book owes a great deal to many people, beginning with both our families and community of friends – too many to name – who made our sudden return home hospitable and comforting, providing room, sourcing furniture, and sharing meals and love. We are grateful especially for all your support and companionship through the pandemic lockdowns. To our son Harvey, who made the confines of home a wonderful and fun refuge amidst the chaos and challenged us to be our most creative, patient, and sacrificial selves – this work is part memento of the precious early years we spent together.

We are grateful for the opportunity given by our editorial team at Routledge to produce this book as a documentation of this historical event, the Covid-19 pandemic. We owe a debt of gratitude to the many researchers and journalists whose work we reference and discuss.

Finally, this work would not have been possible without each other. It is borne of countless invigorating conversations and observations at mealtimes and safely distanced adventures taken around the city during those quiet Covid-19 years.

1 Port in Stormy Seas

As we respond to the pandemic and work towards recovery, we look to our cities as hubs of community, human innovation and ingenuity. Today, we have an opportunity to reflect and reset how we live, interact and rebuild our cities.
— António Guterres, Ninth Secretary General of the United Nations[1]

The gateway to immunity has taken almost three years to open. The Covid-19 pandemic has disrupted economies, placed huge strain on healthcare systems, and caused significant physical and emotional suffering for many across the world. Yet the impacts of the crisis have not been equally distributed across communities.

Leading global cities such as New York, London, and Singapore have been disproportionately affected by the pandemic. Deeply embedded in and highly dependent on the global political economy, global cities have found themselves vulnerable to both the healthcare and socio-economic impacts of the crisis, as infections enter through global travel and trade dwindles on the back of a massive decline in global demand.

Having risen with the tide of global economic growth over the past few decades, global cities now face the stormy seas of global economic decline and uncertainty. Once infection enters a global city, infection clusters tend to spread rapidly, overwhelming hospitals and forcing policymakers to initiate economically costly lockdowns. From a global phenomenon, a pandemic very quickly becomes a domestic and urban issue. As we will show in the rest of this book, the responsibility of mitigating problems that are brought about by a pandemic tends to fall heavily on the shoulders of urban planners, 'street-level' policy officers, and grassroots-level civic organisations.

This is exacerbated by the fact that an infectious disease, once having entered the boundaries of a global city, tends to spread most rapidly *within* cities that possess high population densities and overcrowded marginalised communities. The intermingling of global and local dynamics in a global city – global spread of infectious diseases but urban responses to the localised impacts of these diseases – has led urban scholars to suggest an 'urban

DOI: 10.4324/9781003142553-1

political pathology' that accelerates the spread of infectious diseases among highly connected networks of global cities and which gives rise to rapid institutional decay and degradation once such diseases take root within the city (Keil and Ali, 2011).

We find this notion of urban political pathology to be useful for understanding the spread and management of pandemics in global cities. Like individuals, global cities can 'catch' an infectious disease through exposure to other cities, with the disease subsequently wreaking havoc within the internal systems and structures of the city. Should a cure or sound treatment plan not be forthcoming, a city can easily face 'multiple organ failure', especially in terms of a decline in socio-political institutions, an overwhelmed public healthcare system, deep economic decline, and strains to public infrastructure. A pandemic is therefore more than simply a matter of public health; it is a social, economic, political, and inevitably, urban problem as well.

However, not all is bleak. Like individuals, global cities can also mount a response to the disease, with its capacities and resources mobilised to 'fight' the disease. Contact tracing can be initiated to identify and quarantine infected carriers of the disease, nurses and doctors mobilised to treat those who have been infected, and state resources directed to maintaining the functioning of the economy and public infrastructure. More importantly, as we put forth in this book's central argument, a city's immunity can be built up before an infectious disease even enters its borders.

In subsequent chapters, we discuss how urban planners and policymakers can build up urban resilience by acquiring and storing up the various policy capacities that are typically needed at the onset of a pandemic. This could be financial resources, technical expertise, human capital, institutional functionality, or even political trust. But we shall not jump ahead of ourselves. It suffices for now to say that the Covid-19 pandemic is a highly 'urban' pandemic, with its effects particularly pronounced within urban cores and governments' responses to it taking place at an equally urban scale.

An Urban Pandemic

Even the very origin of the COVID-19 pandemic is urban. Wuhan, where the pandemic is believed to originate, is a second-tier Chinese city of economic significance. Cities remain at the forefront of the world's struggle with the Covid-19 pandemic, with a significant proportion of infections emanating from cities, often spreading to city-fringe and rural regions.

According to United Nations Secretary General António Guterres:

> Urban areas are ground zero of the COVID-19 pandemic, with 90 per cent of reported cases. Cities are bearing the brunt of the crisis – many with strained health systems, inadequate water and sanitation services, and

other challenges. This is especially the case in poorer areas, where the pandemic has exposed deeply rooted inequalities.

(Guterres, 2020)

This urban aspect of the Covid-19 pandemic is further iterated by United Nations Assistant Secretary-General Haoliang Xu, who noted in a speech that:

COVID-19 has been largely an urban crisis. Nearly 90% of all cases and epicentres of the pandemic across countries are in cities. But population density does not necessarily correlate with high incidence of the pandemic, but poverty and deprivation, poor planning, inadequate infrastructure and weak governance structures do.

(Xu, 2020)

Given its origination from cities, as well as its continued proliferation within and across urban centres, it is by no stretch of the imagination that we can conceive of the Covid-19 pandemic as, ultimately, an 'urban pandemic'. The urban spread of the Covid-19 pandemic is therefore more than simply a factor of urban density; it is also hastened by the vast global network of cities, most of whom form crucial nodes of international trade and travel (Hall, 1966; Sassen, 2001, 2011). To speak of an urban pandemic is therefore to conceive of it as a phenomenon that impacts both inner-city dynamics and inter-urban relations.

However, this urban nature of Covid-19 extends beyond its emergence and spread. The Covid-19 pandemic is also deeply urban in another way. Specifically, solutions and innovations for tackling the pandemic are also emerging from among the world's leading cities.

As Secretary General Guterres (2020) has observed, 'cities are also home to extraordinary solidarity and resilience. . . . [W]e look to our cities as hubs of community, human innovation and ingenuity'. Such arguments form the backdrop for the recently released United Nations Policy Brief on COVID-19 in the Urban World, which promotes equitable and sustainable urban growth and capacity-building among local governments as key drivers of success in global efforts to manage and mitigate the impacts of Covid-19.

In this book, we will seek to understand the Covid-19 crisis as an urban pandemic by focusing on the urban impacts of the crisis as well as the various urban interventions and solutions that have been developed to address the pandemic within the context of Singapore.

Singapore: Global City-State

As a global city-state, Singapore occupies a unique position in the minds of urban scholars and policy scientists alike. While its small geographical confines have necessitated the complete urbanisation of this 724 km² island, its role as an independent sovereign country also provides its government with the financial and military clout of a full-scale nation-state. While it is ranked among the world's top global cities (Kearney, 2019; The Mori Memorial Foundation, 2019; Wardle et al., 2020), Singapore is also known for its economic competitiveness, diplomatic soft power, and military strength (GFP, 2020; IMD, 2020; McClory, 2019; Panda, 2020), all of which are characteristics of nation-states rather than urban centres.

Singapore's unique position as a global city-state is very much a function of its history. Singapore was first founded as a British trading post in 1819 and subsequently established as a British colony in 1824. It would soon be caught up in a regional drive for independence, first by attaining self-government in 1957, and subsequently through a merger with its northern neighbour Malaysia in 1963. Full independence would, however, be foisted upon Singapore in 1965 by dint of a separation from Malaysia that was borne from political ideological differences.

It was at this point that Singapore had to seriously consider the formation of the various trappings of a typical nation-state, that is, a standing military and police force, public healthcare, basic and tertiary education, water supply, and international trade, among others. At the same time, the constrains of its limited physical and population size continued to plague Singapore, along with pressing municipal issues, such as public housing, urban transit, and sanitation. These tensions remain in modern-day Singapore as it grapples with its dual-faceted existence as both nation and city.

This is further complicated by its deep integration in regional and global economies, driven in no small part by its early leaders' decision to 'leapfrog' the region and attract major multinational corporations (MNCs) instead (Lee, 2000; Lim, 2015). Singapore's central position in global circuits of trade and capital flow has since placed it among the world's leading global cities. As early as 1972, Singapore had identified itself as a global city, with then–foreign minister S. Rajaratnam arguing that, as a global city, Singapore could tap on the rest of the world as its economic hinterland (Rajaratnam, 1972).

Singapore therefore occupies a unique position in the world as a 'global city-state'. While it has joined the ranks of leading global cities such as London and New York, it faces a lonely existence as one of the world's few city-states, alongside the Vatican and Monaco. As we will discuss in the rest of this book, Singapore's identity and role as a global city-state has come with significant challenges and opportunities during the Covid-19 pandemic.

Like other densely populated and highly urbanised urban centres, Singapore has proven to be highly vulnerable to the Covid-19 coronavirus. Despite its small population of 5.6 million, the number of Covid-19 infections in Singapore has exceeded 2.7 million to date, although Covid-19-related fatalities remain low at 1,872 (WHO, 2023). A vast majority of these infections occurred within its foreign worker population, most of whom are housed in dense, cramped, and badly managed dormitories (Sim and Kok, 2020). As the experiences of other major urban centres have shown, high urban density can result in greater infection risks.

Aside from infection risks, Singapore's position as a global city also makes it vulnerable to the knock-on social and economic impacts of the crisis. In particular, the steep decline in global trade that had arisen from economic lockdowns across the world, as well as reduced global travel, had caused Singapore to slip into its worst recession since its independence, with its reliance on trade and tourism becoming its Achilles heel in a global environment of reduced demand and limited travel (Tang, 2020). This would pose further knock-on effects such as retrenchments and growing unemployment and reduced domestic demand.

Despite these urban and economic challenges, Singapore has managed to limit the spread of the Covid-19 coronavirus and minimised the economic impacts of the pandemic. Much of this can be attributed to a series of budgets that provided close to S$100 billion for Singapore's Covid-19 response efforts, with the bulk of these funds channelled towards maintaining employment through wage subsidies and financial support for retraining (Ministry of Finance, 2020). It goes without saying that Singapore's extensive pool of financial resources has allowed it to maintain its healthcare system capacity and carry out the extensive contact tracing that would prove critical for managing Covid-19 infection risks.

These substantial financial resources reflect the availability of national-level resources and capabilities, most notably in the form of Singapore's national reserves (Woo, 2020a, 2020c), that can be mobilised quickly through its national-level political processes and institutions (Woo, 2020b). In short, Singapore has been able to mobilise nation-state levels of resources and capacities to address its urban-municipal and local economic challenges. This is a point that has frequently been emphasised by scholars who have identified Singapore's national-level resources and development strategies as sources of urban competitiveness (Calder, 2016; Guo and Woo, 2016; Low, 2006; Olds and Yeung, 2004; Yeung and Olds, 1998).

In short, Singapore's unique position as a global city-state means that it possesses the strategic nimbleness of a city, accessibility to global markets, and national-level resources and planning processes, all of which have contributed to its pandemic response efforts. However, Singapore's dual identify as global city and nation-state has not come without its tensions and challenges. These will be discussed throughout the rest of this book. At this point, however, it is necessary to first discuss Singapore's model of governance and approach to urban planning, both of which form the backdrop to our subsequent discussions on Singapore's urban response to Covid-19.

Policy and Governance

Singapore's model of policy and governance is very much shaped by its British colonial history. At the heart of this model is Singapore's Westminster parliamentary system, which it inherited from British rule but subsequently introduced a slew of reforms in order to enhance parliamentary representation and responsiveness. These include the introduction of group representation constituencies (GRCs) that require voters to select from different slates of candidates, non-elected members of parliament (MPs) in the form of nominated members of parliament (NMPs) and non-constituency members of parliament (NCMPs), as well as a popularly elected president.

While NMPs are appointed by the president to represent underrepresented segments of Singaporean society, such as the arts and the social sector, NCMPs are 'best-performing' opposition candidates who may have lost in a general election but have nonetheless secured the largest vote shares among all losing candidates. Singapore's Constitution allows for a maximum of 12 NCMPs less the number of elected opposition MPs, with NCMPs enjoying the same voting rights as fully elected MPs. The NCMP scheme was therefore introduced to ensure a minimum number of opposition MPs in parliament, especially in the event that no opposition candidates are able to win a seat.

The most important parliamentary reform for the purposes of our discussion in this book is the elected presidency. While the office of the president had existed as a public figurehead since Singapore's independence, it was in 1991 that the Constitution was amended to provide for a popularly elected president who would serve to safeguard Singapore's national reserves and ensure the integrity of its public service by holding veto power over the use of past reserves[2] as well as the appointment of key public servants. As we will show in later chapters, President Halimah Yacob played a crucial role in approving the government's decision to draw from its past reserves to fund its Covid-19 response efforts.

Aside from its political system, Singapore also retained much of the British civil service model. The various functions of government are therefore performed by different ministries, with each ministry led by an elected minister. Reporting to the minister is the permanent secretary, who represents the top-ranking civil servant within each ministry, as well as other junior political appointees known as ministers of state or senior ministers of state. As was the case with its political system, several reforms were also introduced to enhance the responsiveness and competitiveness of Singapore's civil service.

First, a range of statutory boards were created in order to attract more qualified candidates from the private sector. These statutory boards were given semi-autonomous status, especially with regards to hiring and promotion practices, although each statutory board remains under the purview of a ministry. For instance, the Health Promotion Board is accountable to the Ministry of Health, and the Economic Development Board to the Ministry of Trade and Industry, so on and so forth.

The key difference between ministry and statutory boards was that the latter was frequently able to offer better remuneration packages and greater work flexibility to its employees, even as they continue to play key roles in public service delivery (Lee, 1975; Woo, 2014). Taken together, Singapore's ministries and statutory boards are known as its 'public service', with their employees collectively known as public servants. Employees of ministries, however, continue to be identified as civil servants, with the 'civil service' existing as a subset of the 'public service'.

A third, albeit less formal, component of public service delivery in Singapore are its government-linked companies (GLCs). Often known as state-owned enterprises, these GLCs are usually formed through the corporatisation and privatisation of existing statutory boards, although more recent GLCs have also been formed as corporate entities form the start. Almost all GLCs are either wholly owned or majority-owned by the state, usually through its sovereign wealth fund Temasek Holdings.

In most instances, GLCs are created to provide key public services, such as utilities and public transport (albeit through market mechanisms), and/or provide strategic services, such as military technology. Examples of key GLCs in Singapore include the national carrier, Singapore Airlines; military technology firm Singapore Technologies; telecommunications provider SingTel; rail operator SMRT; and utilities company Singapore Power, among many others.

Forming the final component of Singapore's model of policy and governance is its grassroots and social sector. Two major types of organisations exist within this space, with both involved to varying extents in the provision of public services, especially at the ground level. The first set of organisations are known as 'grassroots organisations' (GROs). Led by the para-political organisation People's Association, GROs are managed by volunteers and serve to provide social assistance and welfare to citizens at the community level (People's Association, 2015).

Of particular importance are the Residents Committees (RCs) and Citizens' Consultative Committees (CCCs), which form a direct link between citizens and the government by implementing the government's assistance schemes for the needy and hosting 'meet the people' sessions (MPS). The MPS takes place on a weekly basis in every constituency and is led by the elected MP of that constituency, who typically addresses residents' needs and concerns in person during these sessions.

As we will discuss later in this book, the grassroots sector plays an important role in Singapore's efforts to manage the social impacts of the Covid-19 pandemic. These efforts involved a significant extent of urban intervention, particularly given GROs' roles in managing municipal issues. GROs therefore play an important role in Singapore's social and urban policy landscape by implementing some of the government's social policies and managing municipal issues at the community level.

Aside from GROs, voluntary welfare organisations (VWOs) also play an important role in fostering ground-up initiatives that serve the social policy goals of the government. These VWOs include charitable organisations, philanthropic trusts, and smaller not-for-profit organisations that serve different segments of society. Underpinning the work of these VWOs is the Ministry of Social and Family Development's (MSF) 'Many Helping Hands' approach that sets the legal, regulatory, and financial parameters within which VWOs operate.

Under this framework, the state provides legal and financial resources while VWOs offer social assistance directly to beneficiaries. The rationale for this approach was that VWOs would be able to respond more quickly to the needs of beneficiaries, given their close contact with the various segments of society (Tai, 2016). As we will also show throughout this book, VWOs played a critical role in driving the various ground-level urban and social interventions that would serve to blunt the impact of the Covid-19 pandemic on citizens.

Hence, despite its caricaturisation as a 'soft' authoritarian state that governs through heavy state intervention (Barr, 2014; George, 2017; Ortmann, 2011; Rodan, 2008; Tan, 2012), there is, in reality, a diverse ecosystem of actors and stakeholders who are involved in the 'co-creation' of policies in Singapore, such as political and para-political organisations, public agencies, corporations, and civil society actors (Singh, 2017; Soon and Koh, 2017; Woo, 2015b, 2019).

However, and especially in the realm of urban planning, the Singaporean state continues to be the dominant policy actor, with public agencies and political leaders setting the policy agenda and formulating policies while non-state actors such as firms and VWOs are involved in policy implementation and evaluation (Woo, 2016, 2018). We will now turn our attention to Singapore's urban planning process, which forms the contextual framework for understanding Singapore's urban responses to the Covid-19 pandemic.

Urban Planning

Formal efforts at urban planning in Singapore first began in 1822, when the British colonial government, under the advice of the settlement's chief engineer and land surveyor, Philip Jackson, introduced its first city plan, known as the 'Jackson Plan' (Chew, 2009). Despite such early efforts at town planning, the British government would take a relatively laissez-faire approach to town planning in Singapore, with formal urban planning only initiated in 1951, on the back of rapid population growth and the emergence of overcrowded slums in the city centre (National Library Board, 2014).

Urban planning from then on has very much been driven by top-down state policy processes. As Yuen (2009: 363) has noted, Singapore is a 'highly planned city-state . . . in which land development is planned and strictly controlled. With few exceptions, all development involving construction or change of use requires permission'. As Yuen goes on to note, 'Singapore presents a prototype of urban governance in which land use planning is taken seriously and plans are implemented with relatively high compliance with development control and planning regulations' (Yuen, 2009: 363).

Certainly, this pervasive role of the state in urban planning and governance comes with pros and cons. While Singapore's urban liveability and quality of life have improved by leaps and bounds, its urban landscape has also
been criticised for its monotony and lack of aesthetic diversity, in no part
due to the orderly and coordinated nature of Singapore's urban planning processes (Yuen, 2009: 381). Another consequence of Singapore's highly centralised urban governance model is an inevitable consolidation of authority in
the state, giving rise to criticisms of elitism and (semi)authoritarianism (Ho,
2016; Kong and Woods, 2018; Tan, 2008).

These trade-offs and criticisms aside, Singapore's urban planning processes have given rise to significant enhancements to its urban environment
and infrastructure. Singapore's success in urban planning has also given rise
to strong global interest in its urban innovations, with the Singapore government often engaged to assist in the planning and development of existing and
emerging cities across East and Southeast Asia (Kolesnikov-Jessop, 2010).

At the pinnacle of Singapore's urban planning processes is the Urban
Redevelopment Authority (URA), which exists as a statutory board under
the Ministry of National Development. The URA therefore serves as Singapore's main urban planning unit by providing guidance and leader-
ship for land use and urban development policies. Broadly speaking, the
URA takes a long-term perspective to urban planning. Its urban planning
approach broadly includes setting broad strategies, identifying the land
needs of various stakeholders, and planning for the necessary infrastructure
and resources needed for these proposed land uses (Urban Redevelopment
Authority, 2016).

The URA's planning process is broadly comprised of two main components:

- *Long-term plan.* A long-term land use plan that guides Singapore's urban,
  land use, and transportation development over the next 40 to 50 years. The
  long-term plan is reviewed and updated periodically.
- *Master plan.* A medium-term land use plan that translates the broad, long-
  term strategies that have been set out in the concept plan into more detailed
  plans for implementation over the next 10 to 15 years. The master plan is
  reviewed every five years.

Both the concept plan and the master plan are ultimately implemented through
the Government Land Sales programme, which releases state land for development in accordance with the URA's planning strategies and guidelines
(Urban Redevelopment Authority, 2016).

Long-Term Plans

Prior to 2021, Singapore's long-term plans were known as 'concept plans',
with the first concept plan introduced in 1971 to address the infrastructure

needs of post-independence Singapore. It therefore included plans to develop new housing estates, industrial estates, transport infrastructure, and recreational spaces across the island, as well as establish the central business district, which would form the core of Singapore's downtown area (Urban Redevelopment Authority, 2020c).

Singapore's rapid socio-economic development in the 1970s and 1980s would prompt the formulation of Concept Plan 1991, which proposed the development of cultural, commercial, and technological corridors that would support Singapore's increasingly technology-oriented economy and its growing population (Urban Redevelopment Authority, 2020c).

For instance, satellite commercial centres were proposed to alleviate congestion in the city centre, while technology clusters would serve to generate greater innovation by bringing business parks, science parks, and academic institutions into closer proximity with each other. Seven low-lying islands were also amalgamated into Jurong Island through land reclamation, allowing for the creation of a petrochemical hub on this island.

Concept Plan 2001 would continue to focus on Singapore's ongoing socio-economic development by planning for a high-quality living environment through a wider diversity of housing options, setting aside land in the city centre to support the growth of Singapore's financial services sector, and enhancing Singapore's recreational spaces through the creation of more parks, reservoirs, and natural areas (Urban Redevelopment Authority, 2020c). A key characteristic of Concept Plan 2001 was a public consultation exercise that collected and incorporated the views of key stakeholders.

More recently, Concept Plan 2011 was reviewed in 2011–2013 and plans for a population range of 6.5 to 6.9 million by 2030. Under Concept Plan 2011 is the Land Use Plan 2030, which includes broad strategies to provide affordable homes with a full range of amenities, ensure greater transport connectivity and urban liveability, as well as sustain a vibrant economy with good jobs (Urban Redevelopment Authority, 2020a). More detailed plans for the implementation of these broad strategies were subsequently included in Master Plan 2014 and Master Plan 2019.

In 2021, the URA embarked on a review of its long-term plan. The review was organised along four central themes:

- Future of the environment
- Future of living
- Future of mobility
- Future of work

At this point of writing, the URA has completed phase 1 of its long-term plan review, with urban liveability and climate change emerging as key issues of concern to participants (Urban Redevelopment Authority, 2022).

Master Plans

Master plans are statutory land use plans that provide guidance for Singapore's development over the next 10 to 15 years. Reviewed every five years, master plans serve to translate concept plans into detailed plans for guiding the development of land and property. Singapore's first master plan was approved in 1958 and focused on improving housing, reducing overcrowding and traffic congestion in the city by developing satellite towns, and reserving land for industrial development (National Library Board, 2014). The master plan has subsequently been reviewed and revised to address Singapore's emergent social, economic, and urban needs.

These iterations include Master Plan 1980, Master Plan 2003, Master Plan 2008, Master Plan 2014, and Master Plan 2019. The most recent master plan review culminated in the gazetting of Master Plan 2019, which focused on providing inclusive, sustainable, and green neighbourhoods with ample community and recreational spaces, as well as the rejuvenation of heritage zones and areas (Urban Redevelopment Authority, 2020b). An important feature of Master Plan 2019 is the inclusion of detailed plans for the development of underground spaces in the districts of Marina Bay, Jurong, and Punggol (Malone-Lee, 2019).

Aside from the concept plan, Master Plan 2019 also drew from the report of the Committee on the Future Economy, an economic policy committee that was formed to identify and develop Singapore's future industries and sectors (Committee on the Future Economy, 2017). Given the report's focus on innovation and Industry 4.0, Master Plan 2019 included plans to develop 'enterprise districts' such as Punggol Digital District, with greater flexibility of land use and space planning introduced in these districts (Malone-Lee, 2019).

As our discussion thus far has shown, Singapore's position as a global city-state has led it to adopt a unique approach to urban policy and governance that, while highly centralised and state-centric, nonetheless involves a broad range of state, non-state, and quasi-state actors. In the rest of this book, we will flesh out how this broad range of actors has given rise to diverse urban interventions that were implemented in response to the Covid-19 pandemic.

Overview of the Book

With the current chapter having provided a broad understanding of Singapore's approach to policy, governance, and urban planning, Chapter 2 will provide a more in-depth review of the existing literature on urban planning and pandemics. Of particular interest in this chapter are the existing research and studies that have been conducted on the role of urban planning in governments' pandemic response efforts, as well as the impacts of pandemics on urban planning processes across the world.

We will then delve into the first major policy intervention that was adopted by Singapore in response to the Covid-19 pandemic: social distancing and the 'circuit breaker', a de facto lockdown. Aside from the obvious socio-economic impacts, the circuit breaker also prompted significant urban interventions and adaptations that were put in place to ensure social distancing. In Chapter 3, we will document the urban interventions and adaptations that had emerged in response to the circuit breaker.

While the circuit breaker served to minimise social interactions and hence reduce local transmission of the coronavirus among Singapore's resident population, large infection clusters would nonetheless emerge from within Singapore's large foreign worker population, a significant proportion of which was housed within cramped and badly managed dormitories. In order to preserve health system capacity, the Singapore government had to mobilise a range of urban facilities in order to house both healthy and infected foreign workers, in order to reduce the density of foreign worker dormitories.

These facilities include convention centres and holiday resorts that were converted into makeshift 'community care facilities' for infected foreign workers, as well as military camps, schools, and vacant housing complexes that were mobilised to house healthy foreign workers. In Chapter 4, we will discuss the mobilisation of such facilities in terms of 'excess urban capacity'. As we will show in this chapter, the availability of such excess urban capacity played a key role in preventing Singapore's public health system from becoming overwhelmed by this large wave of infections.

In both the implementation of the circuit breaker and the mobilisation of excess urban capacities, the state played a central role. This involved public officials from a broad range of public agencies, as well as personnel from Singapore's military and police force. However, non-state actors, such as volunteer welfare organisations (VWOs), charitable organisations, grassroots organisations, and citizen groups, also played key roles in Singapore's societal response to the pandemic. These efforts range from ground-up initiatives to support marginalised communities to spontaneous urban adaptations to ensure public safety and social distancing.

In Chapter 5, we will discuss such ground-up urban interventions and adaptations and address their impacts on Singapore's social and urban landscape. In doing so, we aim to go beyond statist understandings of urban interventions by discussing the urban nature of ground-up and societal responses to the pandemic. From a broader and policy-centred perspective, the various government and ground-up interventions that emerged in response to the pandemic would ultimately feed back into Singapore's urban planning processes.

In June 2020, the URA announced that it would be reviewing its urban plans, including Master Plan 2019, to factor in new urban needs that have arisen due to the Covid-19 pandemic. Potential changes include introducing more mixed-use neighbourhoods into the central business district, larger public spaces that facilitate social distancing, and greater capacity in social amenities and food-and-beverage outlets. In Chapter 6, we will discuss these emerging changes to Singapore's urban plans and provide a rough sketch of Singapore's urban future in a post-Covid-19 landscape.

Notes

1 Statement by António Guterres on the impact of Covid-19 in Urban Areas. 28 July 2020. (*BINUH*, 2020)
2 Reserves that have been accumulated by previous terms of government.

2 Urban Policy and Pandemics

Given their high levels of density and the propensity for face-to-face interactions, cities have proven to be highly vulnerable to the spread of infectious diseases (Hamidi et al., 2020). Urbanisation can affect the epidemiological characteristics of infectious diseases, whether in terms of the speed or nature of the spread of an infectious disease (Alirol et al., 2011). Urban centres have therefore been described as 'catalysts' for the rapid spread of infectious diseases (Neiderud, 2015). This is further compounded by the highly interconnected nature of cities, with infectious diseases spreading not only *within* but also *across* cities through international travel and migration.

Yet despite this vulnerability of global cities to pandemics and the tendency for infectious diseases to spread rapidly within densely packed urban centres, urban planning as a field and scholarly endeavour does not sufficiently address issues of public health and epidemiology. Indeed, there is growing recognition of a divide between urban planning and public health (Corburn, 2004, 2007; Hoehner et al., 2003; Kent et al., 2018).

But this was not always the case. In many developing societies, the initial aims of urban planning have tended to focus on improving sanitation and preventing disease outbreaks. For instance, public health and urban planning co-evolved in late 19th-century America due to a need to reduce the harmful effects of rapid industrialisation and urbanisation, such as poor sanitation, air pollution, and dangerous working conditions, all of which tended to accelerate the spread of diseases such as cholera and typhoid (Corburn, 2004: 541).

Major urban planning initiatives in Singapore have often been motivated by similar concerns. For instance, the post-independence introduction of mass market public housing was stimulated by the crowded and unsanitary slums that much of its population was living in. These slums were hotbeds for infectious diseases, such as cholera, tuberculosis, and malaria. They also posed severe fire safety hazards, with the disastrous Bukit Ho Swee fire of 1961 being a strong case in point.

These efforts to remove slums and rehouse citizens were made in tandem with a mass immunisation programme, with the cumulative outcome being a sharp decline in number of deaths due to communicable diseases (Lee Kuan

DOI: 10.4324/9781003142553-2

Yew School of Public Policy, 2019). Urban planning and public health were therefore often seen as complementary endeavours, during the initial stages of a city's development, that can contribute to the health and safety of the population.

However, as knowledge of diseases advanced and cities achieved higher levels of urban development, the professions of urban planning and public health experienced a sharp split, with the control of infectious diseases achieved through medical interventions such as antibiotics and vaccination and the urban planning increasingly focused on economic and commercial concerns (Greenberg and Schneider, 2017: 12–21).

From an urban perspective, this gave rise to urban sprawl and suburbanisation; a growing reliance on automobiles that ironically restricted access to health services for children, the disabled, the elderly, and the poor; and as well as the concentration of pollutive industrial activities in select districts and neighbourhoods (Greenberg and Schneider, 2017: 19). These problems have prompted some urban planners and urban scholars to rethink the impacts of their work on public health outcomes.

However, urban planning has also been seen by some as a key contributor to positive public health outcomes, whether in terms of reducing the spread of infectious diseases or promoting healthier lifestyles among citizens (Glaeser, 2012; Sarkar et al., 2014). Certainly, the Covid-19 pandemic has prompted more urgent efforts among policymakers to rethink their approach to urban planning, with the aim of designing cities that can be more resilient in the face of future pandemics. Scholars are calling for greater efforts among urban planners and architects to include pandemics and other healthcare crises in their disaster management strategies and urban designs (Allam and Jones, 2020).

From this perspective, effective urban planning can contribute to pandemic preparedness and response. We will now turn our attention to existing work on how urban planning can help contain and manage the effects of a pandemic.

Planning for Pandemics

Broadly speaking, urban centres are typically better equipped to handle a pandemic. Through better housing and living conditions, improved sanitation, and readily accessible health and social services, more developed cities tend to experience lower mortality rates during a pandemic and are better able to curb the spread of infectious diseases (Alirol et al., 2011; Hamidi et al., 2020; Neiderud, 2015). This is despite the fact that cities also tend to be more densely populated than their suburban or rural counterparts.

Hence, while urban density can make cities vulnerable to the initial spread of an infectious disease, such density can paradoxically also allow for more effective pandemic control measures. For instance, the case of Singapore has shown how densely populated cities can allow for more efficient contact tracing and surveillance efforts (Woo, 2020a). As Neiderud (2015: 1) has noted, 'city planning and surveillance can be powerful tools to improve the global health and decrease the burden of communicable diseases'.

Furthermore, urban density allows for significant economies of scale in the provision of social and medical services, with a certain number of healthcare institutions planned for each district or neighbourhood. This is not to say that all cities are equally well-planned. Certainly, urban slums in less-developed countries such as India have thrown up major challenges for policymakers, with informational gaps and unsanitary living conditions frustrating governments' efforts to manage the spread of the coronavirus within these communities (Friesen and Pelz, 2020; Golechha, 2020).

In any case, it is increasingly clear that sound urban planning can contribute significantly to a city's ability to respond to pandemics and manage the spread of infectious diseases. While well-planned cities have shown a remarkable extent of resilience to the Covid-19 pandemic, badly planned cities have shown how planning gaps can exacerbate the crisis. Moreover, pandemics have often given rise to tectonic shifts in governments' understanding of and approach to modern urban planning.

Urbanisation has been described as a concerted effort to 'plan and manage our way out of infectious diseases' (Bereitschaft and Scheller, 2020; Klaus, 2020), with cholera in 19th-century London and typhoid in 20th-century New York frequently cited as instances whereby the spread of an infectious disease gave rise to significant implications for urban planning, such as modern sewer systems and water treatment facilities or the establishment of zoning codes and health boards to ensure access to healthcare.

Urban planners can therefore play an important role in ensuring that cities are better designed to manage the impacts of an infectious disease outbreak. For instance, Matthew and McDonald (2006) have argued that urban planners can prepare for a major epidemic by working with public and private groups involved in disaster planning, designing land, and transportation planning information systems to aid and support decision-makers during a crisis, encouraging greater self-sufficiency in food production and consumption, designing realistic evacuation strategies and routes, and considering the impacts of their daily planning recommendations on disease risk and response.

More broadly speaking, scholars have called for more centralised planning and decision-making processes alongside greater sensitivity to local and ground-level needs and dynamics (Ahsan, 2020; Woo, 2020a). In light of the Covid-19 pandemic, UN-Habitat has, in its Report on Cities and Pandemics (UN-Habitat, 2020), advocated for several planning principles to ensure better urban health as well as to prevent future pandemics:

- Ensuring better access to healthy food, clean air, water, and sanitation
- Reducing overcrowding and planning for adequate density
- Planning for '15-minute neighbourhoods' that facilitate quick access to amenities during a lockdown

- Encouraging the development of sustainable local economies
- Providing cities and local governments with more resources
- Encouraging greater coordination within and across governments at different levels
- Increasing public sector capacity and encouraging digitisation in government

At a more micro level, specific planning processes and interventions have been shown to help reduce the spread of infectious diseases. For instance, restrictions on household overcrowding and the provision of more parks and open spaces can help reduce urban density and relieve congestion, both of which are known to exacerbate the spread of diseases transmitted through respiratory routes (Alirol et al., 2011). Less relevant to Covid-19 but nonetheless still important is the need to ensure access to safe drinking water, which helps reduce the spread of waterborne diseases (Alirol et al., 2011).

The needs of public health institutions and disaster response mechanisms can also be considered and incorporated into zoning and design processes, while building designs should aim to 'de-densify' in order to allow for greater physical distancing (Ahsan, 2020: 284). This last point was made particularly salient by the Covid-19 pandemic, with social distancing employed as a key policy tool for reducing the spread of the coronavirus. As we will show in later chapters, initial efforts to contain the spread of the virus in Singapore involved extensive urban interventions and adaptations that were aimed at encouraging social distancing and enforcing it.

Aside from urban planning processes, smart city technologies have also been identified as tools that can contribute towards a city's pandemic readiness efforts. These include the use of artificial intelligence for better healthcare monitoring and surveillance (Hossain et al., 2020; Yigitcanlar et al., 2020), advanced data systems that allow for more efficient processing and dissemination of information (Costa and Peixoto, 2020), and deep learning and video surveillance technologies for monitoring social distancing in public areas (Shorfuzzaman et al., 2021), among many others.

Kummitha (2020) has found that countries that extensively employ smart city technologies in their Covid-19 response efforts have been able to limit the transmission of the coronavirus more quickly, with China being a strong case in point. As we will discuss in the rest of this book, smart city technologies such as artificial intelligence and data analytics have also played an important role in Singapore's Covid-19 response by contributing to its contact tracing and healthcare system monitoring processes (Baharudin, 2020; Woo, 2020a, 2020c).

Smart city technologies therefore represent an important set of tools that city planners can draw upon to support their cities' pandemic preparedness and resilience efforts. However, it is important to note that technology should not be seen as the panacea for addressing pandemics. As Kummitha (2020) has further noted, the political and institutional context of a country or city can affect the implementation of technological tools and shape human–technology interactions.

One important socio-economic variable is urban inequality, with urban slums and poorer neighbourhoods particularly susceptible to the spread of infectious diseases due to overcrowding, material deprivation, low rates of literacy and education, lack of healthcare access, and insufficient immunisation (Alirol et al., 2011). Urban and healthcare interventions should therefore pay attention to these socio-economic situations and contexts, with the ultimate aim of reducing their prevalence.

There is therefore a need for a broader and more inclusive approach to urban planning that integrates the technological or technical aspects of planning with the socio-political and institutional context within which this planning takes place. We argue that a focus on resilience can provide such a broad framework for ensuring that urban planning and governance are better geared towards pandemic and disaster response.

Risk and Resilience in Urban Planning

Black swan events such as the Covid-19 pandemic are, by definition, unpredictable and unanticipated. If the nature and timing of a black swan event could be determined ahead of time, it would no longer be a black swan event.

Scholars have long identified resilience to be a useful framework addressing and managing threats that are unknown, unquantifiable, systemic, and catastrophic (Baum, 2015; Capano and Woo, 2017; Klein et al., 2003). Indeed, a sizeable proportion of the existing research on resilience is focused on the management of socio-ecological threats such as natural disasters and climate change (Adger, 2000; Adger et al., 2005, 2011; Berkes and Folke, 2003; Cavallo and Ireland, 2014; Folke et al., 2002, 2010; Stewart et al., 2009; Klein et al., 2003).

According to Vale (2014: 191), resilience can be thought of as:

- A theory for explaining how systems behave across scales, whether these are neighbourhoods, subnational hinterlands, or even multinational regions
- A practical approach to planning systems across social spaces
- An analytical tool that allows researchers to examine how and why certain systems are more capable of responding to disruptions

In their survey of the literature on resilience in public policy processes, Capano and Woo (2017) have identified two different forms of resilience:

- Resilience as 'rebounding' from shock and returning to a prior equilibrium state
- Resilience as retaining functionality during shocks and crises

These two forms of resilience were first identified in the seminal work of C. S. Holling, who thought of *resilience* as 'the persistence of relationships within a system and is a measure of the ability of these systems to absorb changes' and, simultaneously, 'the ability of a system to return to an equilibrium state after a temporary disturbance' (Holling, 1973: 17).

However, much of this early work tended to conflate the two – absorbing changes and returning to equilibrium – without considering the possibility that these two processes may occur independently of each other. In other words, it is entirely possible, and even necessary, for a system to absorb changes and transition to a new equilibrium point that may be entirely different from pre-crisis conditions (Capano and Woo, 2017, 2018).

Given the vulnerability of cities to major threats and disruptions, there has naturally been growing interest among urban scholars on notions of 'urban resilience' or the 'resilient city'. As Vale has noted, the application of resilience to urban studies introduces a greater strategic focus to urban planning and design. These include 'preventive' and 'anticipatory' designs that involve investments in different parts of the built environment in preparation for potential disruptions.

As Vale has noted, there are deep socio-political considerations to some anticipatory urban resilience. Who decides which locations and communities are vulnerable to risks and hazards (and, hence, worthy of investment)? What happens to communities that are displaced as a consequence of such efforts to strengthen or enhance certain aspects of the built community? There is therefore a need for a 'more holistic view of anticipatory resilience' that takes into account the full range of affected parties and locations (Vale, 2014: 194).

Such socio-political considerations aside, Eraydin and Taşan-Kok (2013) have pointed out that resilience thinking can contribute to urban planning by:

- Facilitating a greater understanding of the interrelated nature of socio-economic and ecological systems
- Emphasising the adaptive capacity of socio-ecological systems
- Understanding the impacts of external and non-systemic factors on urban systems
- Providing a basis for the systemic analysis of cities and their vulnerabilities
- Understanding how ecosystem services can improve human well-being
- Encouraging the building of urban capacities

The last point of urban capacity-building is particularly relevant to this book, with Eraydin and Taşan-Kok (2013) arguing that 'changes will take place, and while trying to reduce the risks, urban systems should be prepared to absorb these changes, reorganise themselves and develop new adaptive strategies to manage and cope with the change while sustaining their main functions'.

From this perspective, resilient cities are seen as 'complex adaptive systems' that draw on interlinkages between local communities and the environment in responding to social, economic, and environmental changes (Mehmood, 2016: 407–408). As we will discuss in later chapters, such interlinkages played a key role in Singapore's response to Covid-19, with ground-up initiatives by VWOs and citizen groups serving to enhance neighbourhoods' ability to cope with the pandemic.

From an urban planning perspective, Davoudi et al. (2013) have delineated resilience into four main dimensions:

- Preparedness: the capacity to learn
- Persistence: being robust
- Adaptability: being flexible
- Transformability: being innovative

Under this schema, cities

> can become more or less resilient depending on their social learning capacity (being prepared) for enhancing their chances of resisting disturbances (being persistent and robust), absorbing disturbances without crossing a threshold into an undesirable and possibly irreversible trajectory (being flexible and adaptable) and moving towards a more desirable trajectory (being innovative and transformative).
>
> (Davoudi et al., 2013: 311)

Covid-19 and the City: Urban Implications and Responses

There is little doubt that the impacts of the Covid-19 have been most severely felt in major urban centres that tend to be densely populated and deeply embedded within the broader global economy. Whether it is New York, London, Tokyo, or Paris, major cities across the world have faced an onslaught of Covid-19 infections. This has brought forth great strain to their healthcare systems and public infrastructure. At this time of writing, New Delhi is experiencing a major surge in Covid-19 infections and fatalities.

It is also notable that the Covid-19 virus is most commonly thought to have originated from Wuhan, a major 'tier two' city in the Chinese province of Hubei. As we had discussed in Chapter 1, the initial spread of the coronavirus also took place across major and secondary cities. While the Covid-19 pandemic has since engulfed the entire world and entered all major territories, there is little doubt that the emergence and initial spread of the coronavirus involved densely populated cities.

At the same time, and as we will discuss in the rest of this book, the innovative solutions and technological tools that have been developed to help governments combat the pandemic have also mostly been developed by research institutes, entrepreneurs, and firms that are located within major cities. An OECD policy report has noted that:

> Cities are on the frontline of responses to the COVID-19 crisis. They play a key role to implement nation-wide measures, but also provide laboratories for bottom-up and innovative recovery strategies. COVID-19 accelerated the shift towards **a new urban paradigm** towards inclusive, green and smart cities.
>
> (OECD, 2020)

Urbanisation, therefore, is a double-edged sword, and cities can be at once both catalyst and panacea for major global crises. As the previously cited OECD report has also pointed out, major crises such as the Covid-19 pandemic can also give rise to important paradigmatic change to the urban form and urban thinking. In the rest of this chapter, we will provide an overview of the emerging literature on the impacts of Covid-19 on cities and urban policy, as well as the urban responses that have been mounted to combat the crisis.

Urban Implications

The Covid-19 pandemic has revealed the extent of cities' vulnerability to the spread of infectious diseases. This is also certainly not the first time that cities have faced the brunt of a major pandemic, as examples such as the 1665 Great Plague of London, New York's experience with the 1918 Spanish flu, and the more recent 2003 severe acute respiratory syndrome (SARS) outbreak in Hong Kong can attest. However, there has been surprisingly very little research done on this link between cities and pandemics (Sharifi and Khavarian-Garmsir, 2020).

Indeed, much of the existing literature has focused on the impacts of natural disasters and climate change to cities (Downey, 2017; Mera and Balijepalli, 2020; Pelling, 2012; Sanderson, 2000), with subsequent efforts to develop urban system resilience consequently focused on natural disaster response and climate change mitigation (Mera and Balijepalli, 2020; Norris et al., 2007; Pelling, 2012; Vale, 2014).

While these studies have no doubt contributed to cities' crisis response and resilience-building efforts, there remains a lacuna in our understanding of how pandemics impact cities and how cities ought to build up their resilience to global pandemics.

While there have been efforts to meld urban policy with public health (Greenberg and Schneider, 2017), much of this has focused on encouraging the formation of 'healthy' cities and well-being through the provision of more green spaces or the creation of infrastructure for bicycles and cycling (Corburn, 2013; Harpham et al., 2001; Joassart-Marcelli et al., 2011; Petersen,

1996). While these interventions can no doubt help encourage greater public health in better-designed and more sustainable cities, little is said about how cities should respond to major public health crises such as a global pandemic.

The limitations of these well-meaning efforts have led some urban scholars to lament the growing divide between urban policy and public health (Corburn, 2004, 2007; Greenberg and Schneider, 2017). Nonetheless, the Covid-19 pandemic has given rise to a flurry of research on the impacts of the pandemic on urban systems.

In their review of early research on the impact of Covid-19 on cities, Sharifi and Khavarian-Garmsir (2020) identify four major themes around which this research is clustered, namely, environmental quality, socio-economic impacts, management and governance, and transportation and urban design. However, Sharifi and Khavarian-Garmsir also note that this emerging body of work is heavily skewed towards the theme of environmental quality, with the other three themes relatively underexplored.

This focus on environmental quality is particularly salient in urban dwellers' heightened demand for urban green and blue spaces as well as other private or communal outdoor spaces during the pandemic, with these spaces in turn helping to mitigate the negative impacts of COVID-19 on the quality of life in many cities (da Schio et al., 2021; Mayen Huerta and Utomo, 2021; Mouratidis, 2021; Yamazaki et al., 2021).

These findings have led urban scholars to advocate for more equitable access to urban green spaces and better-designed urban green spaces that can provide a range of amenities for urban dwellers (Lopez et al., 2021). Urban sustainability and pandemic resilience intersect in other ways as well. Paradoxically, the lockdowns that were instituted in response to Covid-19 infections have also given rise to improvements in air quality in many cities, giving rise to significant reductions in pollutants such as NO_2, SO_2, and CO as well as levels of PM_1 and PM_{10} (Clemente et al., 2022; El Kenawy et al., 2021; Gamelas et al., 2021). The same can be said for urban heat, with reductions in traffic during lockdowns or reduced urban mobility resulting in significant declines in surface temperature and heat island effects (Teufel et al., 2021).

Urban Responses

While the pandemic has given rise to severe implications for urban centres, city governments and urban policymakers have responded to the crisis with varying degrees of success. While cities such as Hong Kong, Singapore, and Taipei have managed to 'flatten the curve' and reduce community transmission of the Covid-19 virus to near-zero levels, others such as New Delhi continue to grapple with soaring Covid-19 cases and increasingly taxed healthcare systems.

In almost all instances, successful city-level responses to Covid-19 have been predicated upon the presence of integrated urban governance systems that facilitate long-term planning, adequate investment in primary healthcare systems, and effective coordination of multiple sectors and stakeholders (Earl, 2020; Sharifi and Khavarian-Garmsir, 2020; Woo, 2020b). This is particularly the case with the four 'Asian Tigers' of Hong Kong, Singapore, Taiwan, and South Korea, all of whom had developed effective crisis and pandemic response processes due to their experience with the 2003 SARS crisis (Hartley and Jarvis, 2020; Her, 2020; Lee et al., 2020; Summers et al., 2020; Wan et al., 2020; Wang et al., 2020; Woo, 2020a).

Indeed, and as we will discuss in later chapters, Singapore's response to the Covid-19 pandemic was driven by its highly centralised and integrated approach to urban policy and crisis management, with the government's Multi-Ministry Taskforce for Covid-19 directing the pandemic response efforts of public agencies, firms, grassroots organisations, and citizen groups. Urban governance is therefore an important determinant of success for governments faced with an emergent infectious disease outbreak.

In this book, we include both state and non-state actors in our conception of urban governance, with NGOs and grassroots organisations playing important roles alongside policymakers and planners in Singapore's Covid-19 response efforts. Effective urban responses to the Covid-19 pandemic therefore requires a significant extent of adaptability and responsiveness among urban planners, policymakers, and citizens.

This is particularly the case in cities which have found their healthcare systems overwhelmed by large numbers of Covid-19 infections. In these cases, there has been a need to modify and adapt existing urban spaces and infrastructure in order to create more healthcare facilities. In many cities, convention centres and exhibition halls were swiftly converted into makeshift hospitals and patient care facilities. We will discuss Singapore's efforts to create such facilities in Chapter 4.

In the Chinese city of Nanjing, a 1,500-room hospital was built over the span of five days in January 2021 to help contain Covid-19 cases in the region (CNA, 2021). This is not the first time that China would build an entire hospital in a matter of days. In February 2020, an emergency hospital equipped with 1,000 beds and 30 intensive care units was built in Wuhan over the course of ten days (Ankel, 2020).

In all these instances, city governments have responded to the pandemic – particularly the strains that the pandemic has placed on healthcare systems – by mobilising vast amounts of resources and construction capabilities to create new healthcare facilities, whether by modifying and adapting existing urban infrastructure or creating new hospitals from scratch. In doing so, these cities have made extensive – and often permanent – changes to their urban landscapes and public health systems.

Aside from such large-scale urban developments, the Covid-19 pandemic has also prompted city governments to make micro-level adjustments to their urban landscapes. These include inserting Covid-19 testing centres and vaccination centres within communities that are accessible to residents and allow for sufficient social distancing while these residents are either tested or vaccinated for Covid-19. A particularly prominent example is South Korea's 'drive-through' testing centres. As we will discuss in later chapters, Singapore has set up Covid-19 testing and vaccination centres across its regional hubs and neighbourhoods. In many instances, grassroots organisations were mobilised to assist in these efforts, with vaccination centres set up in community centres and residents' committees acting as important channels of information as well as source of ground-up initiatives.

Another important enabler of urban responses to the Covid-19 pandemic has been technology. This is particularly the case in smart cities with access to cutting-edge data analytics and artificial intelligence technologies that could be quickly applied to pandemic response efforts. For instance, China has used robotics, autonomous systems, and artificial intelligence to enforce social distancing and manage quarantined individuals (Chen et al., 2020a). Urban analytics was also employed in Hangzhou, with GIS mapping used to identify initial outbreaks and DBSCAN used to identify infection clusters (Li et al., 2021). In Singapore, the government drew on artificial intelligence and data analytics to enhance its contact tracing and healthcare resource management processes (Woo, 2020c).

This use of digital technology to enhance and expedite contact tracing was similarly reported in Taiwan, alongside the use of data analytics to integrate healthcare system databases with its immigration and customs database to facilitate the identification of potential Covid-19 cases by generating real-time alerts on a recent patient's travel history during clinical visits (Summers et al., 2020; Wang et al., 2020).

In analysing the use of technology in governments' Covid-19 response efforts, Kummitha makes a distinction between a top-down 'techno-driven' approach that uses technology to discipline citizens' behaviour and compliance with Covid-19 measures and a 'human-driven' approach that focuses on public education and government–citizen communications (Kummitha, 2020). As we will discuss in later chapters, both approaches can be found in the case of Singapore.

Urban Resilience

Having discussed the urban impacts of, and urban responses to, the Covid-19 pandemic, we are now in a better situation to discuss the contours of urban resilience in a post-Covid world. Certainly, urban resilience is by no means an entirely new subject. Cities have, for millennia, borne the brunt of disease, disaster, and decay. Yet despite these trials and tribulations, many cities have rebounded and regained their positions in the global economic order.

One only needs to consider the histories of London and Boston, both of which have survived major plagues and outbreaks of infectious diseases. For an even more salient example, we should cast our eyes further back to Ancient Greece – to be precise, Athens, which has survived plague, warfare, and occupation to become what is broadly known as the cradle of democracy.

What makes such cities resilience? Why do some cities survive crisis after crisis while others fall into chronic decline? These questions have driven, and continue to drive, the efforts of urban scholars to understand the sources and bases of urban resilience. In terms of urban design, there is an emerging consensus that the way in which a city is designed can significantly affect its vulnerability to an infectious disease outbreak.

In their study of Hong Kong, Kwok et al. (2021) have highlighted the importance of urban geometry in ensuring urban resilience to Covid-19, with spatial factors such as building height, building density, and average street length contributing immensely to a neighbourhood's or district's tendency to give rise to Covid-19 infections. Specifically, high building height and high building density have been associated with poorer wind ventilation and higher risk of infection, while longer average street length facilitated social distancing by reducing social contact and walking mobility (Kwok et al., 2021).

Scholars and researchers have also found strong linkages between urban green spaces and pandemic resilience. This research has found that urban green and blue spaces not only contribute to citizens' sense of well-being (da Schio et al., 2021; Erdönmez and Atmiş, 2021; Lopez et al., 2021; Mayen Huerta and Utomo, 2021; Yamazaki et al., 2021) but also help reduce Covid-19 transmission by shifting urban mobility to outdoor settings such as parks (Johnson et al., 2021; Xie et al., 2020). Furthermore, Herman and Drozda (2021) highlight the importance of less rigidly designed and multifunctional green spaces in contributing to the sort of 'tactical pandemic urbanism' that allows citizens to develop a greater sense of autonomy amidst social distancing.

Taken together, these emerging studies show that the urban form and physical infrastructure of a city can determine its level of resilience to Covid-19 and other infectious diseases by reducing risks of Covid-19 spread and infection and facilitating greater social distancing through specific urban designs. However, it is also important to note that aside from urban space and infrastructure, urban culture and demographic can also impact a city's resilience to Covid-19.

In a study of the ultra-orthodox Jewish community in Israel, Hananel et al. (2022) find that greater urban diversity is associated with lower rates of infection, with greater variations in a population's day-to-day routines and interactions serving to reduce risks of infection. This suggests a need to incorporate a greater extent of urban diversity through specific urban interventions that influence or take into account the daily spatial practices of local populations. A useful example of such interventions is Singapore's existing ethnic integration programme, which sets strict quotas on the ethnic mix of its public housing estates.

It should, however, be noted that relationships between urban diversity and Covid-19 infections are also highly dependent on the socio-cultural context of the city in question. For instance, Huang and Li (2022) have found in their study of New York City that neighbourhoods with a higher concentration of Asians tend to exhibit lower infection rates, while those with higher concentrations of Blacks, Hispanics, elderly, uninsured, poor, and large households have higher infection and death rates.

Hence, depending on the socio-cultural make-up of a neighbourhood, urban diversity affects infection rates in different ways. There is therefore no linear relationship between urban diversity and infection rates that is applicable across all cities and contexts. In light of this, Huang and Li argue that location-specific interventions will be required for managing future pandemics and reducing health disparities within and across cities (Huang and Li, 2022: 12).

Despite this emerging effort to identify key sources of vulnerability, as well as key drivers of resilience, to the Covid-19 pandemic, it is also clear that urban resilience is a function of multiple variables, none of which can, on its own, provide a definitive or even convincing account of what makes a city resilient. Just as successful and thriving global cities are more than a sum of their urban infrastructure and demographics, urban resilience depends on a confluence of multiple factors, the result of which is an often-immeasurable 'X factor' that animates urban life and sustainability in leading global cities across the world.

As the urban economist Edward Glaeser has pointed out:

> The long view of urban resilience suggests that cities are far more vulnerable to economic and political dislocation than to earthquakes, wars and even pandemics. The most consequential catastrophes are those that fragment existing institutions and economies, which is why the strength of civil society determines the consequences of any disaster. The COVID-19 pandemic is dangerous for the world's cities because it has exacerbated existing challenges, including adapting to virtual life and the political instability associated with growing urban discontent.
>
> (Glaeser, 2022: 4)

In the following chapters, we will discuss the myriad sources of risk and vulnerability that Singapore faced in its early experience with Covid-19, as well as the multiple drivers that have together driven the city-state's response to, and recovery from, the most deleterious impacts of the pandemic.

3 Till Sickness Do Us Part

Social Distancing and Lockdowns

Like most coronaviruses, the Covid-19 coronavirus spreads through airborne droplets that are expelled when an infected person coughs, sneezes, and talks and which enter the respiratory systems of people who may be in close proximity. For this reason, Covid-19 infection control typically involved ensuring adequate physical distance among individuals as well as the mandated wearing of face masks, both of which aim to reduce the spread of droplets from an infected person to others in close contact.

The maintenance of physical distance is often referred to as 'social distancing'. According to the WHO, social distancing involves keeping a distance of at least 1 m from other people, as well as avoiding crowded places or spending time in groups (World Health Organisation, 2021). The US Centers for Disease Control and Prevention (CDC) similarly states that:

> Limiting close face-to-face contact with others is the best way to reduce the spread of coronavirus disease 2019. . . . To practice social or physical distancing, stay at least 6 feet (about 2 arm lengths) from other people who are not from your household in both indoor and outdoor space.
>
> (CDC, 2020)

In Singapore, the term that is used for the maintenance of such physical distance is 'safe distancing' rather than 'social distancing', while the distance that is kept between individuals abides by WHO recommendations of 1 m. We will use the two terms interchangeably throughout the rest of this book, although *safe distancing* will be used when discussing the context of Singapore and *social distancing* to refer to the broader global understanding of maintaining physical distance to prevent the spread of Covid-19.

As we will also discuss in the rest of this chapter, *social distancing* is more than simply a matter of keeping a 1 m distance between individuals. It also encompasses a broad range of rules and regulations that determine the number of individuals that can gather in groups, as well as the ways in which groups and individuals are expected to occupy and use public spaces. Social distancing therefore involves adaptations to the urban and physical environment that

DOI: 10.4324/9781003142553-3

facilitate the movement and gathering of individuals without compromising on social distancing rules.

In many instances, this has involved very specific spatial rules and instructions, such as demarcations on the ground to indicate where one should stand or sit.

Safe distancing was first introduced on 13 March 2020, when the MOH issued social distancing requirements and advisories for events, gatherings, workplaces, and public venues. These advisories include requiring dining venues to set seats as least a metre apart, entertainment venues and sport centres to enforce limits on number of visitors, and employers to implement telecommuting, staggered work hours, and the spacing out of workstations and seats in meeting rooms (Ministry of Health, 2020a). It was therefore at this stage that the basic guideline of maintaining 1 m apart from other individuals was first introduced.

Safe distancing measures would be further tightened on 20 March 2020, with the MOH requiring all operators of venues which are accessible to the public to ensure a 1 m distance between patrons; this includes placing floor markers or demarcations to ensure patrons queue at least a meter apart from each other and marking out alternate seats in food and beverage venues where seats are fixed and cannot be removed (Ministry of Health, 2020d). The safe distancing measures that were announced on 20 March 2020 would therefore

Figure 3.1 Floor markings in the Changi City Point mall indoor atrium demarcating permissible standing and sitting zones.

Source: Debbie R. Loo.

Figure 3.2 In the initial months of the lockdown, all public dining was prohibited.
Source: Debbie R. Loo.

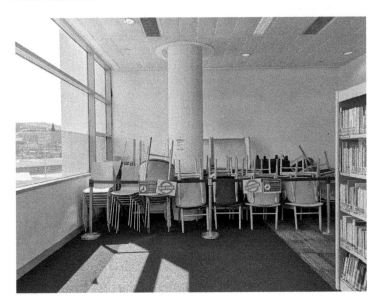

Figure 3.3 Lingering in public civic spaces like public libraries was also prohibited.
Source: Debbie R. Loo.

give rise to enduring adaptations to Singapore's urban landscape, such as floor markings and seats that are marked out for safe distancing purposes.

These measures would only be rolled back more than two years later, on 26 April 2022, when Singapore formally removed all safe distancing requirements. By regulating the physical location of physical bodies as well as the flow of crowds in public spaces, safe distancing would significantly affect not only the ways in which public spaces were planned and organised but also the nature and intensity of interaction among individuals and between humans and their urban environs. This impact of social distancing on the urban space and urban dynamics has not gone unnoticed by scholars of urban studies.

Social Distancing and Urban Dynamics

For urban planners and users of urban spaces, social distancing presents an existential dilemma. Cities thrive on urban density and the dynamic social interactions that such density affords. This is especially the case for major global cities and business hubs that have long been driven by the concentration of businesses and consumers within a circumscribed area.

Known in urban studies as 'agglomeration', this concentration of business and human interactions, lubricated by the support of 'advanced producer services' such as legal services and accountancy, has allowed the major global cities of today to become key command-and-control centres of an increasingly globalised and disaggregated world economy (Sassen, 1999, 2001, 2011).

Agglomeration and clustering have also been identified as key drivers of innovation, another important determining factor of urban economic development and global city formation (Carlino and Kerr, 2015). Urban density has, in fact, been positively correlated with higher productivity and innovation (Carlino et al., 2007), with measures of innovation such as patent intensity rising in tandem with employment density, the latter of which is also a function of urban density (Duranton and Puga, 2020).

Given their strategic locations and the presence of technology, talent, and infrastructure, global cities such as London, New York, Singapore, and Hong Kong have successfully positioned themselves as the confluence of global flows of trade, money, people, and ideas, in the process becoming leading global financial centres, business and maritime hubs, and smart cities (Sassen, 2011; Taylor, 2000; Wardle et al., 2020; Woo, 2015a, 2018).

However, there are also downsides to such heightened urbanisation and economic globalisation. Global cities are often buffeted by global crises and instabilities. For instance, the 2007 global financial crisis resulted in massive recessions in many global cities, driven by a global credit crunch. More recently, the Covid-19 pandemic has disproportionately impacted global cities more severely, with all the advantages that these cities possess rapidly turning into double-edged swords.

For instance, the openness of many global cities had facilitated the import of infected persons through their air, sea, and land borders. Subsequent efforts to close off these borders would paradoxically also cut off many cities' access to migrant workers and global talent – essential preconditions of their economic success. Disruptions to global supply chains would also prove deleterious for global cities that have become reliant on these supply chains for their daily needs, particularly for city-states such as Singapore that lack natural resources and hinterland.

Perhaps most tragically, the urban density that had facilitated the dynamic and serendipitous interactions that had driven many urban economies would become a major source of risk, as the Covid-19 virus spreads rapidly among individuals living and working in close proximity. The urban form has therefore become the main battle theatre in the battle against Covid-19, as governments across the world struggle to contain the rapid spread of the virus in major urban centres across the world.

This has led to the widespread implementation of social distancing measures in cities all over the world, with strict controls over physical proximity between individuals as well as the intensity of social interactions in public spaces seen as important tools for minimising the spread of the Covid-19 virus among individuals. While there is little doubt that social distancing has served to reduce infections and 'flatten the epidemic curve' in many jurisdictions across the world (Abouk and Heydari, 2021; Matrajt and Leung, 2020; Milne and Xie, 2020; Moosa, 2020; Qian and Jiang, 2020), it has also been associated with greater social isolation and degradation of mental well-being.

It should, however, be noted that social distancing as a concept is not new, nor is it entirely a matter of pandemic response – whether it is Covid-19 or some past pandemic. The distance between individuals and the social behaviours associated with different distances were first examined by Edward T. Hall in 1966 and given the name *proxemics*. In his seminal book *The Hidden Dimension*, Hall (1966) identified four types of distances:

- Intimate: less than 1.5 ft
- Personal: 1.5 ft to 4 ft
- Social: 4 ft to 12 ft
- Public: 12 ft to 25 ft

According to Hall, intimate distance is reserved for loved ones, whom we share deep relationships with, while personal distance is shared with good friends and family, social distance with acquaintances, and public distance with all others who happen to be around us in a public space (Hall, 1966; Mehta, 2020: 669). In Singapore, *social distancing* is defined as keeping a distance of at least 1 m (or 3.28 ft) from others. The US Centers for Disease Control and Prevention (CDC) advises individuals to maintain a distance of 6 ft from others (CDC, 2020).

Figure 3.4 Floor markings indicating queue positions at a café, while dining in at F&B
was prohibited.

Source: Debbie R. Loo.

Based on Hall's typology of space, social distancing as practiced in both
the American and Singaporean contexts precludes intimate and personal distances, allowing for only social and public distances to be kept. As urban
scholars are becoming increasingly aware, Covid-19 social distancing has
given rise to new forms of proxemics. This has, in turn, resulted in significant
changes in the ways in which individuals and groups interact with their cities
as well as planners' understanding of how urban spaces should be planned and
designed in a post-Covid world.

Safe Distancing in Singapore: Panacea for a Pandemic?

Broadly speaking, safe distancing can be thought of as a suite of rules and
requirements that seek to reduce public and workplace density, with the aim
of minimising sustained close contact between and among individuals and
thereby reducing risks of infection. It is important to note that, in Singapore,
safe distancing affects urban spaces in two key ways. These are related to the
two concepts of urban intensity and urban flows.

First, safe distancing affects the intensity in the use of public spaces
by specifying the distance that is to be maintained between individuals,

particularly when they are dining or in queues. This involves regulating and (as we will discuss later) enforcing the physical location of individuals in a given public space. Second, safe distancing determines the flows of people across and within public spaces. This includes specifying pathways and directionality for pedestrians as well as allowing for single points of entry and exit for public venues.

Safe distancing has been particularly effective as a tool for reducing urban density and intensity in the use of public spaces. This is especially the case with regards to restrictions on the number of individuals who can gather in public or visit each other, as well as the mandated 1 m distance that individuals and groups were to keep from each other. Hence, as infection levels rose in the early stages of the pandemic as well as during the Delta variant outbreak, group sizes were kept to either two or five, depending on the severity of infection levels as well as healthcare systemic capacity.

In order to ensure compliance with safe distancing rules, 'safe distancing ambassadors' and enforcement officers were deployed to patrol public venues and enforce safe distancing rules. Hired as part of the government's short-term employment and relief measures, safe distancing ambassadors and

Figure 3.5 In response to a surge in Covid-19 cases, group sizes of social gatherings were curtailed. Here, tape is used to demarcate boxes that accommodate group sizes of no more than two during the Christmas season of 2021 in the Star Vista mall's naturally ventilated semi-outdoor amphitheatre.

Source: Debbie R. Loo.

Figure 3.6 Safe distancing ambassadors were initially employees from civil service units who were deployed from their regular roles to 'patrol' malls and public venues and ensure the public complied with safe management measures.

Source: Debbie R. Loo.

enforcement officers were authorised to issue warnings and fines to individuals who do not comply with safe distancing rules. Over the span of three years, members of the public who had either lost their jobs due to Covid were employed in this role. This was a temporary paid position which enabled the government to optimise manpower for this long-term measure. Throughout the pandemic, safe distancing ambassadors played a strong role in ensuring safe distancing amongst the public and, as a corollary, reducing urban density in public spaces.

Aside from the 1 m distancing between individuals and groups in public settings, 'safe management measures' were implemented to ensure safe distancing within the workplace. At the broader level, these measures focused on encouraging remote working by restricting the number of employees allowed to be at the workplace and/or the amount of time that they could spend at the workplace. Upon the conclusion of the circuit breaker, 50% of employees were allowed to be at the workplace. Firms were also encouraged to stagger their start times and allow for more flexible working hours.

In order to maintain this 50% workplace occupancy requirement, firms were required to allow their employees to work in the office on a rotational 'split team' basis, with half of the firm's employees working in the office and the other half working remotely. It was also not uncommon for firms and organisations to allow full remote working, with no requirements for employees to return to the office.

These requirements would be relaxed as Singapore's Covid-19 infection rates went down. In April 2021, work-from-home (WFH) requirements were revised to allow up to 75% of employees to be at the workplace, while limits on work hours and amount of time that employees could spend at the workplace were removed. Firms were nonetheless encouraged to allow telecommuting and working from home. In April 2022, all safe management restrictions were removed as Singapore moved into its Covid-19 endemic phase.

In order to manage the flow of people into public venues such as malls, schools, workplaces, and places of worship, as well as to keep track of individuals who enter such public venues, a national digital check-in system known as 'SafeEntry' was implemented across all public venues. SafeEntry was implemented in conjunction with TraceTogether, a Bluetooth-based system that enhanced contact tracing efforts by tracking the individuals with whom one has come into close contact. The MOH defined *close proximity* as up to 5 m apart for 30 minutes (Government Digital Services, 2020).

Under the SafeEntry system, individuals were required to either scan a SafeEntry QR code on their TraceTogether app, which would log their details, such as identification card and mobile phone numbers, in the SafeEntry system. The data collected through SafeEntry would be encrypted and stored in government servers for 25 days. The data can be accessed for contact tracing purposes as well as for criminal investigations and proceedings into seven categories of serious offences.

More importantly, the TraceTogether app displays users' vaccination status. This feature was particularly important when 'vaccination-differentiated safe management measures' (VDS) were implemented, which allowed only vaccinated individuals to enter public spaces such as shopping malls and offices, as well as to dine in at restaurants. Enforcement officers would therefore be able to determine the vaccination status of an individual and either grant or deny access to a public space through the TraceTogether app.

The TraceTogether app was, however, initially not well-received by residents, due to privacy concerns and reports of the app causing users' smartphone batteries to deplete at a faster-than-usual rate (Chong, 2020a). Older and less digitally savvy residents were also hesitant, or simply did not know how, to use the app. In response, GovTech issued physical TraceTogether tokens that similarly relied on Bluetooth technology to keep track of other users in close proximity but which did not require the use of smartphones.

The user of a TraceTogether token would therefore only need to carry the token with them everywhere they went. A barcode that was printed on the token also allowed SafeEntry enforcement officers to scan the token at SafeEntry checkpoints. Enforcement officers could also check the vaccination

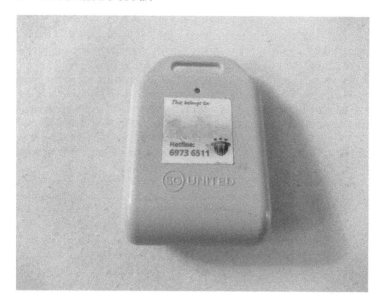

Figure 3.7 TraceTogether token.

Figure 3.8 TraceTogether token dispenser machine at Kitchener Complex.

status of an individual by scanning his or her TraceTogether token. Further regulatory efforts were implemented to ensure widescale use of either the TraceTogether app or token.

Safe Distancing in Singapore's Urban Landscape

Safe distancing would give rise to significant urban adaptations and, in the longer term, leave an indelible mark on Singapore's urban landscape. While some of these urban interventions and adaptations are driven by government mandates and regulations, others were implemented by owners and users of public spaces in order to reduce urban density and ensure social distancing. As we will discuss in the rest of this section, many of these urban interventions and adaptations would significantly reshape the ways in which urban spaces were used and occupied.

This is particularly the case in public venues such as shopping malls, schools, hospitals, and workplaces. In nearly all cases, access to such public venues were restricted to a single entry point. This was to facilitate SafeEntry check-ins and monitoring of crowd levels within the public venue. In public venues where there was greater manpower capacity, multiple entry points were allowed, although the number of entry points remained limited. SafeEntry checkpoints were then set up at each entry point to screen and collect the identifiable details of individuals. This required the venue to station at least one staff member at each entry point.

In many instances, tentage and other temporary structures were erected to provide shelter to both enforcement officers and individuals awaiting entry into the public space.

Sometime in May 2021, automated SafeEntry gantries were deployed in some malls to make access more convenient for the public and reduce the manpower shortage faced by mall management to physically man entry and exit points (Kurohi and Lim, 2021). These installations were also used to regulate crowd numbers, avoid bottlenecks of manual registration, and track and screen out access by public by vaccination status. It also minimised occurrences of disputes between mall staff and safe distancing enforcement officers and the public when entry is denied.

Even as Singapore removed its safe distancing requirements, some public venues have chosen to keep the SafeEntry gantries in place, in the event of another infection spike and/or the return of safe distancing measures.

Within public venues, measures were also put in place to ensure safe distancing among users of public spaces. These include markings on the ground, often through the use of tape, that demarcate the 1 m distance that individuals are supposed to keep from each other, as well as seats and tables that were marked with tape or cordoned off to prevent members of the public from using them. In other settings, cable tie or cordon tape was used to fence off and secure chairs to prevent them from being used by members of the public.

Figure 3.9 Manual SafeEntry point at a mall. In the early days, mall staff were stationed with TraceTogether manual registration procedures. Such measures were also used to comply with occupancy limits of the malls set by authorities under safe management measures.

Source: Debbie R. Loo.

Workplace safe management measures would nonetheless give rise to significant impacts for the city, particularly in city centre office spaces. The prevalence of remote working or 'hybrid working' (which involves a combination of in-office and remote work) has prompted firms to reconsider their office space needs, with some firms vacating or reducing their office spaces in order to reduce rental costs (Lim, 2021). In 2021, DBS announced that it would cut office space across its markets by 20% over the next four to five years, with hybrid work arrangements and a broad redesign of its office spaces reducing its office space needs (Ang, 2021).

More recently, Standard Chartered Bank announced plans to reduce its Singapore office space by half, in the process giving up nine floors of office space in the Marina Bay Financial Centre (The Straits Times, 2022). As it was the case with DBS, Standard Chartered's decision to half its office spaces is predicated upon a long-term shift towards remote working and hot-desking. Such efforts to reduce office spaces have also sparked off a heightened demand for coworking spaces, as multinational corporations downsize their main offices and relocate their workers to coworking spaces instead (Lee and Zalizan, 2022).

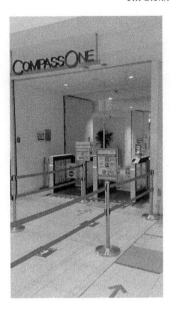

Figure 3.10 Automated SafeEntry gantries. After the roll-out of the TraceTogether app and tokens, automated gantry systems were deployed at malls and large retail shops.

Source: https://commons.wikimedia.org/wiki/File:Automated_SafeEntry_gantry,_2021-09-04.jpg.

Despite these moves to reduce office space, Standard Chartered has maintained that Singapore remains a 'critical global hub' for the bank (The Straits Times, 2022). The de-intensification of office space and the city centre more broadly may therefore not entirely be incompatible with Singapore's global hub ambitions. While agglomeration dynamics continue to attract global banks and corporations to Singapore, post-Covid work arrangements and urban density requirements may paradoxically result in some shrinkage and fragmentation in the city centre, office space demand decline, and coworking spaces proliferation.

Conclusion

In this chapter, we have discussed the urban implications of Singapore's safe distancing measures. While safe distancing has served to reduce infection rates by spacing out individuals and preventing the spread of the virus in overly densely populated spaces, it has also given rise to hitherto unanticipated implications for cities and their urban spaces. At the broadest level, the urban impacts of safe distancing can be thought of in terms of 'intensity' and

Figure 3.11 (a–d) Variety of methods implemented to cordon off public seats and pub-
          lic spaces, such as community centres and hawker centres, to enforce safe
          management measures during different phases.

Source: Debbie R. Loo.

Figure 3.11 (Continued)

'flows'. By requiring a 1 m distance between individuals and groups and mandating capacity limits in public venues, safe distancing significantly reduced the number of individuals who are allowed to enter and use a public space at any point in time.

Aside from intensity, safe distancing also significantly affected the ways in which individuals navigated public spaces. This is most evident in the establishment of SafeEntry checkpoints in public venues, with these checkpoints limiting access to the public venue to a single point of entry. This means that all individuals seeking to enter public venues could only do so through one entry point. As we discussed earlier, this would give rise to crowding or 'bunching' of individuals at these entry points as well as concerns over fire safety rules when single-point entry was implemented and enforced under lock and key without ample consideration for the need of emergency exits (Tan, 2020; *The Straits Times*, 2020).

Even as safe distancing measures have been removed at this time of writing, some of the urban impacts of safe distancing may prove to be more 'sticky' than expected. For instance, some restaurants and cafés continue to maintain safe distancing measures, even as requirements to do so have been removed. For their part, individuals and groups continue to keep a distance from each other. This is despite the fact that ground demarcations and other safe distancing guidelines have been removed. Behavioural patterns associated with safe distancing have proven to be relatively enduring.

The most significant long-term impact of Covid-19 on the city will, however, be focused on the city centre, with remote and hybrid work arrangements likely to reduce office space demand among firms. As we have shown in this chapter, major banks such as DBS and Standard Chartered have already embarked on significant reductions in their office spaces. Firms have also sought to reconfigure their office spaces to facilitate hot-desking and coworking arrangements.

The increase in coworking spaces that is expected to occur in tandem with reduced office space occupancy by major corporations may result in a diversification and fragmentation of Singapore's city centre. Where the traditional image of a global city is one of soaring skyscrapers emblazoned with the names of companies that take up anchor tenancy, the post-Covid city centre may feature instead more coworking spaces and a more diverse mix of tenants within office buildings.

4   Mobilising the City
Urban Infrastructure and Capacity

The surge of Covid-19 cases across the world, exacerbated by the emergence of the highly infectious Delta and Omicron strains, would place significant strains on healthcare systems in many countries and jurisdictions. As infection clusters grew and more individuals came down with Covid-19, hospitals found themselves overwhelmed by large patient loads. This is especially the case for intensive care units (ICUs), with severely ill Covid-19 patients outstripping ICU capacities.

Singapore was no exception. The emergence and subsequent spread of the Delta variant of the virus would cause daily cases in Singapore to surge into the thousands, peaking past 5,000 new daily cases in October 2021 (Ministry of Health, 2022a). Infection rates would surge even further with the onset of the Omicron strain, with daily cases exceeding 15,000 and reaching a high of 25,000 in February 2022 (Ministry of Health, 2022a). When cases of the Delta variant surged in October 2021, Singapore experienced severe strains in its ICU capacity, with Covid-19 ICU occupancy rates peaking at 171 (Yong, 2021).

In response, the Ministry of Health sought to expand the number of ICU beds that were available for Covid-19 patients from 219 to 280, although such efforts were hampered by insufficient healthcare workers who could man the additional ICU units (Yong, 2021). The situation would be less severe during the Omicron strain, with 30 patients warded in ICUs in February 2021, despite daily infection rates exceeding 15,000 during that period (Ministry of Health, 2022b).

In this chapter, we will discuss Singapore's efforts to expand its healthcare capacity by converting existing urban spaces and facilities into temporary healthcare facilities. Such efforts are by no means unique to Singapore. Faced with massive waves of infection and strained healthcare institutions, countries across the world have sought to either build new hospitals and care facilities or convert existing venues and spaces into healthcare facilities.

DOI: 10.4324/9781003142553-4

Urban Facilities as Healthcare Capacity

Strains on healthcare systems, particularly critical care capacity, have been associated with increased Covid-19 mortality. A study of 88 US Department of Veterans Affairs hospitals found that patients who were treated in the ICU during periods of heightened ICU demand faced a near twofold increase in their risk of mortality when compared with patients who were treated during periods of low ICU demand (Bravata et al., 2021). Based on World Bank and Johns Hopkins University data, Khan et al. (2020) have found that greater healthcare capacity was associated with lower incidents of Covid-19 fatality, with every unit of increase in the authors' healthcare capacity index associated with a 42% decrease in case fatality.

The impacts of healthcare system disruptions, particularly those arising from shortfalls of healthcare system capacity, are equally deleterious. A study of 31 health services during the pandemic found that disruptions in health services often preceded Covid-19 waves, with shortfalls in healthcare system capacity likely exacerbating infection waves (Arsenault et al., 2022). The impacts of health service disruption also extended beyond Covid-19 patients, with maternal services, child vaccinations, and screenings for cancer, tuberculosis, and HIV severely affected (Arsenault et al., 2022). These findings are hardly surprising, since any shortcomings in or disruptions to facilities and healthcare staff can severely hamper a hospital's ability to provide timely treatment to severely ill Covid-19 patients.

As Covid-19 cases surged in 2020 and 2021, healthcare systems cross the world would quickly find themselves overwhelmed by the deluge of Covid-19 patients who were seeking medical attention. In more resilient healthcare systems such as Singapore, hospitals remained able to provide treatment and beds to Covid-19 patients even as hospitals found themselves stretched (Baker and Mohan, 2020). In less-resilient healthcare systems such as India, severely ill Covid-19 patients were either left to wait outside or turned away from hospitals that had become overwhelmed by sudden surges in Covid-19 cases (Dhillon, 2021). In any case, healthcare system capacity and resilience have risen to the fore in public health debates.

In response to strains on their healthcare systems, many countries have sought to establish temporary or makeshift healthcare facilities. These facilities often take on three forms: temporary emergency hospitals, makeshift hospitals that are built by transforming existing public buildings and spaces, and isolation or infectious disease wards that are converted from general wards (Li et al., 2022). The earliest Covid-19 temporary emergency hospitals can be found in China during the early stages of the pandemic. In February 2020, two temporary hospitals were constructed within weeks in Wuhan, with each hospital capable of accommodating more than 1,000 patients each (Wibawa, 2020).

Such efforts to build new temporary hospitals from scratch are few and far between, requiring significant amounts of manpower and resources. More frequently, makeshift hospitals are created through the conversion of existing spaces and infrastructure. For instance, a large number of 'Fangcang' shelter hospitals were built, first in Wuhan, and subsequently across China, by converting existing public venues such as stadiums and exhibition centres into healthcare facilities (Chen et al., 2020b). In the northern Italian city of Turin, a concert hall was converted into a temporary emergency hospital for the treatment of mild and moderate Covid-19 patients in March 2020 (Sacchetto et al., 2020). Similarly, a trade and fair and exhibition centre in Madrid was converted into a field hospital with a maximum capacity of 5,000 conventional beds and 500 ICU beds in March 2020 (Valdenebro et al., 2021). More recently, the Omicron wave has led China to build more than 60 makeshift hospitals in anticipation of significantly higher Covid-19 caseloads (Bloomberg News, 2022).

It is also important to note the various infrastructural and design considerations that underpinned the development of many of these makeshift hospitals. Given their large interior spaces, exhibition halls and convention centres are frequently selected to become makeshift hospitals. Furthermore, exhibition halls are, by design, modular in nature, allowing for different configurations of exhibition spaces in accordance with the needs of organisers and exhibitors. Such spatial flexibility and modularity are necessary conditions when converting a public venue into a makeshift hospital (Valdenebro et al., 2021).

More importantly, the Covid-19 virus's mode of transmission requires greater attention to be paid to air treatment and ventilation. For instance, the existence of two separated air treatment units in Turin's Officine Grandi Riparazioni concert hall allowed public health officials to create a light negative pressure area when the concert hall was converted into a makeshift hospital (Sacchetto et al., 2020). The presence of a multi-utility tunnels (MUTs) system in Madrid's IFEMA Trade Fair and Exhibition Centre also allowed for the delivery of medical gases such as oxygen and medical air (Valdenebro et al., 2021).

Aside from air treatment, there is also a need to take into account the logistical aspects of delivering medical supplies and services to makeshift hospitals. In Turin, officials were able to convert the backstage area of the concert hall into an area for the delivery and unloading of medical supplies, while an elevated control booth was used by doctors and nurses to oversee patients (Sacchetto et al., 2020). The IFEMA Trade Fair and Exhibition Centre's MUTs also allowed for the delivery of secure Wi-Fi access to the Madrid digital hospital platform, allowing doctors to access patients' medical records as well as provide hospital services such as CT scans and radiology on-site (Valdenebro et al., 2021).

Given that pandemics involve lengthy periods of treatment and isolation, Covid-19 makeshift hospitals will need to cater for isolation and essential living needs. This differs from makeshift hospitals that are established during natural disasters, which focus on providing swift medical treatment and subsequent evacuation of patients to other hospitals. In their study of Fangcang shelter hospitals, Chen et al. (2020b) identify three key characteristics (rapid construction, massive scale, and low cost) and five essential functions (isolation, triage, basic medical care, frequent monitoring and rapid referral, and essential living and social engagement) of Covid-centric makeshift hospitals.

In sum, it is clear that makeshift hospitals that are established to deal with increased caseloads during a pandemic need to cater to medical needs that differ from those that are required during a natural disaster or other non-medical crisis. These include the need for air treatment systems and quarantine or isolation facilities, features that are particularly important when dealing with an infectious disease that is transmitted through air.

Mobilising Urban Facilities in Singapore

With Singapore being a small city-state with severe land constraints, its healthcare system came under significant strain when infection levels surged in 2020. The ebb and flow of infections over the course of both 2020 and 2021 would offer little respite for Singapore's healthcare system. As the country was faced with these strains and constraints, it was critical for Singapore to expand its healthcare system capacity. In order to do so, the government took a two-pronged approach. First, it sought to ramp up the availability of hospital beds through the creation of community care facilities. Vaccination centres were also set up in community centres and other locations, further reducing the workload of healthcare workers and institutions.

To further encourage and facilitate a wider vaccinated population, the Ministry of Manpower issued an advisory on 23 October 2021 with a 'call to action' by its tripartite partners for employers to 'continue to facilitate vaccination (including vaccination booster shots) by granting paid time-off to employees to receive their shots, and additional paid sick leave (beyond contractual or statutory requirement) in the rare event that an employee experiences a vaccine-related adverse reaction' (*Ministry of Manpower Singapore*, n.d.)

This was complemented by a second set of measures that focused on preventing or minimising the emergence of large infection clusters that threaten to overwhelm the healthcare system. This included creating more spaces for housing foreign workers and quarantining travellers. In both instances, existing urban space and facilities were converted into community care facilities, foreign worker housing, and quarantine facilities. Unlike other larger countries, Singapore possessed neither the space nor the resources and manpower required for building 'greenfield' temporary hospitals from scratch. Rather, a 'brownfield' approach was taken, whereby existing sites and facilities were adapted for Singapore's Covid-19 policy needs.

Figure 4.1 Temporary vaccination centres set up by various private healthcare groups were deployed in neighbourhood community centres, Kebun Baru Community Club (shown), to bring vaccination accessibility into the heartlands.

Source: Debbie R. Loo.

Community Care Facilities

On 24 March 2020, the MOH announced that Covid-19 patients who were well but still testing positive for Covid-19 would be moved to a 500-bed community care facility (CCF) that had been newly set up at D'Resort NTUC, a holiday chalet in Eastern Singapore (Chong, 2020b). The facility was established to help reduce the patient load in Singapore's public and private hospitals, the latter of which had also been recently mobilised to take in Covid-19 patients. More CCFs would be set up in April 2020 as Singapore's Covid-19 cases continued to rise, with one hall in the Singapore Expo convention and exhibition centre converted into makeshift healthcare facilities that could accommodate at the first instance 480 patients who were either recovering from Covid-19 or 'early patients' who had tested positive for Covid-19 but were otherwise physically well (CNA, 2020).

As noted by Chia et al. (2021), the Expo CCFs were modelled after China's Fangcang shelter hospitals, although a key difference was that CCFs were meant to isolate and care for patients with mild or no symptoms; patients with severe symptoms or at risk of deterioration were sent to hospitals instead. By

Figure 4.2 Up until May 2022, satellite community health screening and Covid vaccination facilities were maintained at certain community locations to make these healthcare services accessible and convenient for the public.

Source: Debbie R. Loo.

June 2020, all ten of Singapore Expo's halls would be converted into CCFs, with a capacity to house almost 8,500 beds (Tan, 2021).

This decision was predicated upon several spatial features that facilitated the conversion of Singapore Expo into a CCF, including separate air-handling units within each exhibition hall; existing utilities such as potable water, toilets, electricity, and internet connection; restricted-access road that facilitated patient transfers and traffic control; on-site kitchen facilities that could cater to large numbers of patients; and open-concept design of the halls that allowed easy conversion of internal spaces into makeshift care facilities (Goei and Tiruchittampalam, 2020: 614).

Within the exhibition centre, three distinct zones were set up. Operations and administrative staff were based in a *green zone*, which comprised the command centre staff rest areas and storage rooms, while the halls which housed patients were designated *red zones*; passageways that connected the green and red zones were designated as *buffer zones* (Goei and Tiruchittampalam, 2020: 614; Tan, 2021). Within each hall, partition walls were set up to create private cubicles that could each house one to two patients, along with a 'sickbay' that housed a resuscitation cubicle (Goei and Tiruchittampalam, 2020: 614–617).

In order to protect healthcare workers as well as minimise their workload, several health technology (HealthTech) tools were deployed. These include 'Computer on Wheels' and 'Telehealth on Wheels', which allow healthcare workers to move their laptops and vital signs monitoring kits to patients; an integrated clinical management system and electronic medical records system known as GPConnect, which allowed healthcare workers in CCFs to access Covid-19 patients' record in the MOH's National Electronic Health Record; and a vital signs monitoring (VSM) system that allowed patients to take their own vital signs and submit these electronically to a central VSM dashboard (Chia et al., 2021; IHiS, 2022).

Aside from their spatial features, the successful development of the CCFs also hinged on the government's planning processes. A multiagency task force comprising of MOH officials, public health personnel, healthcare institutions, and other government representatives was set up to facilitate the transfer of staff, equipment, and technology from public and private healthcare institutions to the CCFs (Goei and Tiruchittampalam, 2020: 619). More importantly, the task force allowed the government to engage its various stakeholders and entities to acquire the resources and manpower that would be needed to staff and operate the CCFs. Given the heavy caseload that the public health system was facing, the task force had to turn to other government entities as well as the private sector for assistance.

This included mobilising state-owned investment company Temasek Holdings to provide the necessary resources; infrastructure firm Surbana Jurong to design and outfit the CCFs in Singapore Expo; healthcare entities Woodlands Health Campus and Parkway Pantai, as well as the Singapore Armed Forces medical corps, to provide medical staff; hospitality firm Resorts World Sentosa to provide non-medical care, such as meals and cleaning; and security company Certis CISCO to provide security and enforcement at the venues (Tan, 2021: 19). While many of the initial CCFs would eventually be closed as Covid-19 cases subsided, the subsequent emergence of the Delta and Omicron variants would prompt the government to re-establish CCFs.

This includes the conversion of Connect@Changi at halls 7 and 8 of Singapore Expo into CCFs for Covid-19 patients with mild symptoms and low risks (Toh, 2021), as well as the establishment of CCFs in other locations such as the holiday chalets D'Resort NTUC and Civil Service Club @ Loyang, Tuas South worker dormitory, former Ang Mo Kio Institute of Technical Education, Bright Vision Hospital, and Village Hotel Sentosa (Teo, 2021). In September 2021, nursing homes were repurposed into 'stepped-up CCFs' to house and care for elderly Covid-19 patients whose underlying chronic illnesses or comorbidities may pose threats of severe illness (Ministry of Health, 2021).

In early 2022, in response to the wave of infections owing to the Omicron variant, a Covid-19 treatment facility for children, their caregivers, and the elderly was further set up at hall 9 of Singapore Expo. This featured family rooms that could accommodate up to 600 children and their caregivers and up to 224 beds for seniors (Ganapathy, 2022). With these additions, hospital beds at the Singapore Expo totalled over 2,500, which made it the largest treatment facility in Singapore (Low, 2022).

In sum, the CCFs provided additional healthcare capacity by drawing from urban facilities, manpower, and resources from other sectors, such as the hospitality and exhibition sectors, both of which possessed excess capacity, as events were cancelled, and travel disrupted, during the pandemic. As we also discussed, other urban spaces and facilities were also converted into CCFs, such as hotels, holiday chalets, educational institutions, and nursing homes. Even as Singapore continues its transition into Covid-19 endemicity, it is clear that a large number (and types) of urban spaces can be quickly repurposed into CCFs during a pandemic.

Chalets, hotels, and exhibition spaces are particularly useful, given that travel and events are typically cancelled during a pandemic, giving rise to a natural set of vacant spaces that can be converted into CCFs. As we move forward, there will be a need to design excess healthcare capacity or 'slack' into Singapore's urban landscape, whether this takes the form of buildings and spaces that can easily be converted into CCFs or the creation of more healthcare facilities. As we will discuss in Chapter 6, these considerations have found their way into the Urban Redevelopment Authority's long-term urban planning guidelines.

Isolation and 'Stay-Home' Facilities

Aside from CCFs, there was also a need for Singapore to find spaces that could serve as isolation and quarantine facilities for potential Covid-19 cases. This was particularly important as Covid-19 cases and numbers of Covid-19 close contacts rose in tandem with Singapore's contact tracing efforts. Furthermore, there was a need to manage potential imported Covid-19 cases as citizens and long-term residents returned to Singapore. As it was the case for Singapore's healthcare system capacity, the rising number of potential Covid-19 cases and their close contacts would impose significant strains on Singapore's quarantine facilities, most of which were initially located within healthcare institutions.

In order to understand Singapore's approach to managing imported and potential Covid-19 infections, it is first necessary to clarify the various extents of isolation or quarantine that were introduced at the early stages of the pandemic. For close contacts of confirmed Covid-19 cases, a quarantine order would be issued that required individuals to be transferred to hospitals for testing and isolation. For visitors and returning residents, a 'stay-home notice' (SHN) was typically imposed, restricting travellers to their place of residence for one incubation period.

SHN requirements were first introduced in January 2020 to limit the importation of Covid-19 cases as infection levels rose in countries across the world. Individuals who entered Singapore from a list of high-risk countries were then required to serve a 14-day SHN in a place of residence, such as a hotel or a family member's home. The aim of the SHN was to isolate travellers for one incubation period so as to detect infections and prevent local transmission from travellers. As subsequent variants of Covid-19 featured shorter incubation periods, the SHN period would similarly be reduced. For instance, the SHN was reduced to ten days with the dominance of the Delta variant (Lee, 2021), and seven days when the Omicron variant became the dominant variant (Yong, 2022).

Incidents of household transmissions from persons under SHN and the rapid deterioration of the Covid-19 situation in countries across the world would, however, prompt the MOH to introduce and expand its 'enhanced SHN' requirements, with all Singapore citizens, permanent residents, and long-term pass holders entering Singapore required to serve a 14-day self-isolation at dedicated SHN facilities (Ministry of Health, 2020b). Under the enhanced SHN requirements, all travellers would be transported directly from the airport to the hotels. They would then be required to stay within their rooms for the entire duration of the SHN.

The introduction of enhanced SHN measures would require the government to rapidly expand its SHN facilities, with more than half of Singapore's 67,000 hotel rooms reserved for SHN and infection control measures rapidly deployed at these hotels (Chiew et al., 2020; Ramchandani, 2020). Given that the Singapore government paid for the SHN stay of citizens, permanent residents, and long-term pass holders, Singapore's hospitality industry was sustained by the government's SHN block bookings. In a 2020 report, CGS-CIMB analysts found that hospitality REITs in Singapore enjoyed occupancy rates of over 90% in Q3 due to government contracts and foreign workers displaced by border closures (Ramchandani, 2020).

Hotels that chose not to serve SHN occupants were also able to attract local customers, with occupancies at hotels offering 'staycations' reaching 70–90% on weekends in late 2020 (Ramchandani, 2020). Singapore's quarantine and SHN requirements would be dialled back with Singapore's shift to Covid-19 endemicity, with SHN requirements waived for all vaccinated travellers, while Covid-19 patients were allowed to self-isolate for 72 hours under the Home Recovery Programme and close contacts no longer required to be isolated.

Aside from maintaining occupancy rates and sustaining the hospitality sector, Singapore's enhanced SHN measures inadvertently showed how the city-state's large number of hotel rooms could be quickly mobilised for isolating incoming travellers and returning residents during a pandemic, thereby helping to reduce local transmissions and further serving to preserve healthcare system capacity. As it was the case with the CCFs, hotel rooms that are vacant when travel is cancelled during a pandemic can be thought of as a form of excess urban capacity that can be converted into isolation and quarantine facilities, therefore reducing the risks of local transmission arising from imported Covid-19 cases and helping to preserve healthcare system capacity.

Housing Foreign Workers

Given the cramped communal living conditions of foreign worker dormitories, it was inevitable that large infection clusters would emerge in these dormitories. In April 2020, more than 1,000 Covid-19 cases a day were detected in the dormitories; by the end of 2020, 54,505 out of the 58,320 who had tested positive for Covid-19 were foreign workers living in dormitories (Ministry of Health, 2020c). In order to reduce the density of foreign worker dormitories, the government decided to house some healthy foreign workers in other facilities, such as schools, military camps, university student accommodations, and vacant public housing projects (Phua and Ang, 2020). This aimed to reduce infection levels within the dormitories by allowing workers to space themselves out better and practice social distancing as far as possible.

It was particularly fortuitous that there were 21 vacant Housing and Development Board (HDB) flats in the Red Hill Estate which were awaiting redevelopment; these flats could be quickly refurbished to house healthy foreign workers (Lim, 2020a). Aside from these flats, healthy foreign workers were also rehoused in other state-owned facilities, such as military camps, former schools, and factories (Ang, 2020; Phua and Ang, 2020). Similar to the CCFs, a Dormitory Task Force comprising officers from the Ministry of Education and Outward Bound Singapore was established to lead the rehousing of healthy foreign workers in vacant schools (Ang, 2020).

These moves, according to then-minister for national development, Lawrence Wong, aimed to 'reduce the density of the dormitories but also importantly, to design new dormitories in a way that will be more resilient to public health risks, particularly the risk of pandemics, learning from the COVID-19 experience' (Ang, 2020). Hence, even as healthy foreign workers were rehoused in vacant state facilities, the Singapore government would embark on the rapid construction of more and better-designed foreign worker dormitories.

These include a range of semi-permanent 'Quick Build Dormitories' and permanent 'Purpose-Built Dormitories' (Government of Singapore, 2020). More importantly, these new dormitories were established on the back of a year-long review that culminated in revised standards for foreign worker dormitories that included a cap of 12 residents in each room, more living space per resident, improved ventilation, and more toilets per resident (Kok, 2021). In end 2020, most of the foreign workers would be moved out of many of these facilities and returned to their dormitories as the Covid-19 situation stabilised and more foreign worker dormitories became available (Lim, 2020b).

Singapore's experience with the infection clusters in its foreign worker dormitories has therefore revealed two important lessons for urban planners and dormitory operators. First, there is a need to ensure a sustainable and safe level of density in foreign worker dormitories. Given that these dormitories involve communal living in close proximity, they pose significant infection risks during a pandemic. The same can be said for other communal living facilities, such as military camps and student dormitories, although these did not result in significant infection clusters.

Second, and more importantly for our discussions in this chapter, there is a need for excess urban capacity to handle sudden spikes in infection. For Singapore, vacant HDB flats, schools, and factories provided useful buffer spaces for housing foreign workers as the government sought to expand and improve foreign worker dormitories across the country. Moving forward, future efforts at pandemic readiness will need to include considerations for converting existing and vacant spaces into housing facilities for healthy residents of communal living facilities. This will help reduce infection risks in communal living settings.

Connect@Changi

While our discussions have thus far focused on how Singapore has sought to modify or adapt its urban facilities in response to the pressing needs of the pandemic, it is also important to point out that efforts were also made to adapt urban facilities to facilitate business activities amid the pandemic. For instance, a pilot short-stay facility known as Connect@Changi was set up in February 2021 to allow business travellers to stay and conduct meetings without the need to serve quarantine on arrival (Chew, 2021b).

Converted from hall 7 of Singapore Expo, Connect@Changi featured meeting rooms with airtight glass panels and separate ventilation systems that allowed business travellers and their Singapore counterparts to meet without direct physical contact; it also had 150 guest rooms and 40 meeting rooms (Chew, 2021b). Under these arrangements, business travellers would be transported directly from the airport to Connect@Changi, where they would stay for the duration of their meetings and be tested regularly for Covid-19.

Connect@Changi was developed by a consortium led by Temasek Holdings and which includes the Ascott Limited, Changi Airport Group, Sheares Healthcare Group, SingEx-Sphere Holdings, and Surbana Jurong. While Connect@Changi has since been converted into CCFs, the process of building an ad hoc business meeting venue reflects the importance of providing safe spaces for business transactions and meetings to take place during a pandemic. The design considerations that have gone into developing Connect@Changi will no doubt serve as a possible model for building pandemic-resilient business infrastructure in the future.

Planning for Future Crises: Excess Urban Capacity and Slack

As our discussion in this chapter has shown, the outbreak of a severe infectious disease can impose severe strains on the city. As infection rates surged, policymakers had to create new spaces for treating Covid-19 patients and isolating potential cases. Where under ordinary circumstances cities would thrive on the close interactions that come with urban density, the onset of a pandemic can quickly turn urban density into a severe risk factor and require its diametric opposite: social distance. Efforts at social distancing would, in turn, require space in order that individuals could be better spaced out.

This is particularly the case for Singapore, which, as a city-state, lacks hinterland and space for spreading people out during a pandemic. As we have shown in this chapter, Singapore's land constraints have required it to repurpose a wide range of urban facilities to support its pandemic response efforts. This includes the creation of CCFs in exhibition halls and holiday chalets, mobilising hotels to serve as quarantine facilities, and creating temporary foreign worker housing in vacant flats and schools as well as military camps, container port terminals, and factories (Tee, 2020). As such, there is a need for greater flexibility and 'modularity' in the design, planning parameters, and use of urban facilities and public spaces.

At the same time, while the emergency creation of short-term healthcare facilities, treatment centres, and quarantine facilities serves a critical function, healthcare planners, architects, designers, and policymakers would also have to pre-emptively program excess capacity into its processes and spaces, which can absorb, to some extent, the unpredictable nature of pandemics and the length of time some quarantines require.

Studies have revealed adverse psychological impacts of healthcare quarantine environments within quarantine facilities which affect not just patients but also healthcare workers and other medical staff. Risks include anxiety, depression, and other stress symptoms, which cut across populations in isolation within supervised quarantine facilities or home quarantine (Alfaifi et al., 2022; Alkhamees et al., 2020; Henssler et al., 2021). Therefore, it is crucial to consider the mental well-being and movement and spatial needs of patients and healthcare workers within designated facilities, by providing adequate pockets of restful and calm zones, therapeutic, meditative, or energising outdoor spaces, which enhance recuperation and reduce negative psychological impacts.

Such flexibility was highlighted by Singapore's Ministry of National Development, which emphasised the importance of catering for 'white spaces' and multi-use facilities that can be quickly adapted for other uses during an emergency, with the Ministry exploring ways to include more hotels in its emergency preparedness plans and incorporate more multi-use features in new infrastructure projects (Lam, 2021). As we will discuss in Chapter 6, such design considerations feature in the Urban Redevelopment Authority's long-term plan, which guides Singapore's urban development for the next 50 years.

Beyond Covid-19, there is a need to take a more considered and systematic approach to converting public venues into healthcare facilities during a healthcare crisis. As Marinelli has noted, the development of makeshift hospitals through the conversion of public venues is an important aspect of 'infrastructure futureproofing', which she defines as 'the process of making provision for future developments, needs or events that impact on particular infrastructure through its current planning, design, construction, or asset management processes' (Marinelli, 2020: 67).

Chen et al. (2020: 1,312) have similarly argued that future design and construction of large public venues such as stadiums, convention centres, exhibition halls, gymnasiums, and warehouses should include features that allow their conversion into makeshift healthcare facilities, such as interior equipment that can be rapidly removed, entrances that are large enough for hospital beds, and ventilation systems that reduce the risk of cross-infection. In any case, Singapore's experience with converting Singapore Expo and other spaces into CCFs also means that these spaces already possess the attributes that can allow them to easily be converted into healthcare facilities during a future outbreak.

However, it is also important to note that no two pandemics are necessarily the same. Policy responses and urban interventions that are implemented in response to pandemics may differ accordingly. For instance, Goei and Tiruchittampalam (2020: 620) have pointed out that Singapore's CCFs may not be as effective in pandemics where case fatality ratios are higher and the disease more virulent and severe; in these cases, patients will require treatment at acute care hospital, and out-of-hospital treatment will no longer be suitable.

5 Ground-Up Urban Interventions

In our discussions so far, we have placed our focus almost overwhelmingly on the role of the state. Specifically, we have discussed the roles of urban policy, social distancing, and urban infrastructure in Singapore's response to Covid-19. Whether in terms of the mobilisation of urban infrastructure and excess manpower or the implementation of safe distancing rules and the circuit breaker, government policy has been a crucial driving force in Singapore's rapid response to the pandemic.

However, Singapore's ability to respond swiftly to the Covid-19 outbreak, as well as to manage the social impacts of the pandemic, have also depended on the role of non-state actors such as grassroots organisations, civil society groups, businesses, foundations, and even ordinary citizens. In most of these instances, the mobilisation of resources or manpower and their application to pressing social or policy needs took place at the ground level. In the Singaporean context, this 'ground level' typically includes neighbourhoods or districts as well as public venues such as shopping malls and hospitals. It is therefore important to consider the role of civil society in driving or enhancing governments' pandemic response efforts.

The onset and severity of the Covid-19 pandemic have given rise to substantial civil society action in many countries, with research in this area growing in tandem as scholars seek to document and understand the role of civil society in Covid-19 policy response efforts. For instance, Cai et al. (2021) have found that civil society played a key role in fostering social resilience in China, Japan, and South Korea during the pandemic by soliciting donations of money and medical supplies, providing social services, disseminating information, and advocating for marginalised groups, in the process reinforcing the respective governments' policy efforts as well as filling in any institutional gaps or voids that may have existed.

It has been noted that the complex nature of state–civil society relationships also means that pre-pandemic relationships – whether adversarial or complementary – can be exacerbated or magnified during the pandemic (Dayson and Damm, 2020). While the pandemic has, in some instances, resulted in the proliferation of civil society activity and the fostering of government–civil

DOI: 10.4324/9781003142553-5

society collaboration (Brunet et al., 2021; Jeong and Kim, 2021; Miao et al., 2021), it has, in other instances, prompted efforts by the state to co-opt or dominate the civil society space (Hu and Sidel, 2020; Kövér et al., 2021; Kumi, 2022).

In instances where government capabilities or policy capacity is lacking, such as the oft-cited case of Hong Kong, civil society can nonetheless play a major role in driving societal responses to the pandemic as well as supporting vulnerable or marginalised segments of society (Hartley and Jarvis, 2020; Wan et al., 2020; Wong and Wu, 2021). In such instances, civil society takes on the bulk of Covid-19 response efforts, at times supplanting the state. Certainly, such instances are atypical, as are cases of complete state dominance or co-optation of civil society. In most cases, a middle ground is often struck between state and civil society, with the two seeking out collaborative arrangements that can serve to enhance and support government interventions.

This is illustrated in Figure 5.1, which shows how state–civil society relations are related to the strength and autonomy of the state and civil society. At one end of the extreme, a strong and vibrant civil society coupled with weak state capacity can give rise to a dominant civil society that provides public services and guidance directly. This is somewhat reflective of the case of Hong Kong. In this rather extreme scenario, the autonomy of civil society – defined as the ability of CSOs to protect themselves from the influence of either state or market actors (Kövér, 2021) – is relatively strong.

On the other hand, a combination of a strong state and weak civil society will result in top-down state-centric approaches, with the government setting the agenda and driving policy implementation. Possessing limited to no autonomy, civil society in this scenario will not be able to insulate itself from state or market forces and will hence either embed itself as part of the state's policy apparatuses or find itself increasingly isolated from the policy process. This is very much the case in China, where its 'zero-Covid' approach continues to hold sway despite resistance from some business and societal actors.

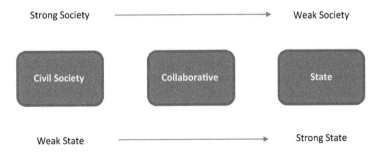

Figure 5.1 State–civil society dynamics.

The ideal situation would lie somewhere in between, with a balance struck between the state and civil society and collaborative arrangements fostered that could allow for an integrated pandemic response effort. Cases such as Singapore and South Korea reflect this balanced approach, with civil society actors playing important roles within the government's broader strategic framework and policy direction. In the case of Singapore, the government's 'Many Helping Hands' framework is a good example of this balance, with the Ministry of Social and Family Development (MSF) providing broad direction and financial resources and civil society tasked with engaging with, and disbursing MSF funds to, the needy (Rozario and Rosetti, 2012).

Hence, rather than thinking about Covid-19 response efforts in a binary state-versus-society manner, it is more important to take an integrated approach that considers how governments and societal actors can collaborate and coproduce policy outcomes. This is particularly relevant to Singapore, where the boundaries between state and society or state and industry can sometimes be (deliberately) blurry, with overlaps between policy actors and non-state actors serving to complement more traditional state-centric means and channels of policymaking (Woo, 2014, 2019).

Civil Society and Grassroots

A key driving force of Singapore's civil society is its grassroots sector, which is led and driven by the People's Association (PA) – a statutory board under the Ministry of Culture, Community, and Youth[1] that comprises a network of over 2,000 grassroots organisations (GROs), 100 community clubs, and 5 community development councils (People's Association, 2015). Of all these grassroots organisations, community centres (CCs) and residents' committees (RCs) played particularly prominent roles during the pandemic.

For instance, mask distribution centres were established in CCs and RCs across Singapore, with volunteers from the grassroots sector, public service, and citizenry helping to distribute masks to citizens (Ministry of Finance, 2022). In February 2020, 200 RCs were mobilised to distribute more than five million masks to local households across Singapore (Tay and Zhang, 2020). Aside from mask distribution, a large number of CCs were also converted into vaccination centres during Singapore's mass vaccination drive in 2021. This involved the setting up of partition walls to provide privacy for individuals receiving their vaccines and waiting areas that could accommodate large numbers of citizens awaiting their turn to receive the vaccines.

More importantly, the involvement of the grassroots sector in Covid-19 response efforts gave rise to significant adaptations to Singapore's urban landscape, particularly at the neighbourhood level. Given their accessibility and central locations within neighbourhoods, RCs and CCs in ordinary time serve as spaces where residents could gather for recreational and community-bonding activities. This accessibility and centrality would prove useful during

Figure 5.2 Bishan Community Club plaza. A permanent sheltered event plaza is adapted into an interim vaccination centre's waiting area.

Source: Debbie R. Loo.

the pandemic, as citizens could collect their masks or receive their vaccines at RCs and CCs that were not only accessible but familiar as well.

Furthermore, the design of many CCs facilitated their conversion into vaccination and mask distribution centres. Many CCs house large open sporting facilities such as badminton and basketball courts which could be adapted into waiting and queue areas. This allowed the orderly administration of vaccines. Backstage areas of auditoriums and other rooms within CCs could also be used to store vaccine and mask supplies, allowing for greater logistical efficiency. Going forward, CCs and RCs will continue to play crucial roles in Singapore's urban life and landscape, both as nodes of social capital and community development during ordinary times and centralised venues for distributing aid and necessities during a crisis.

Aside from the grassroots sector, it is also important to note the role of non-state organisations from Singapore's broader civil society space. In many instances, ground-up initiatives by civil society organisations (CSOs) involved adaptations to or reappropriation of the urban environment.

For instance, Food Bank Singapore established automated food pantries across Singapore that distributed food to the needy by collecting close-to-expiry food items from beneficiary organisations (Food Bank Singapore,

Figure 5.3 Kebun Baru Community Club. An interim vaccination centre's tented waiting area is set up at the basketball court.

Source: Debbie R. Loo.

2020). Food from the Heart is another CSO that solicits food donations and delivers food packages to needy families and students. Given the spike in demand for food among the needy during the pandemic, both organisations played key roles in redistributing food from where they were in abundance to where they were needed across the city. In the case of Food Bank Singapore, the food pantries and vending machines that were set up have become a permanent fixture in many neighbourhoods across Singapore.

Given the infection clusters that emerged within foreign worker dormitories and the subsequent lockdown of many of these dormitories, much of civil society action during the pandemic would focus on providing for the needs of foreign workers living in these dormitories. This includes efforts by CSOs such as the Collective for Migrant Efforts (COME) and Transient Workers Count Too (TWC2) and others to provide food, essential supplies, and internet connectivity to foreign workers. These efforts were significantly bolstered by the creation of platforms and forums – both online and offline – to connect CSOs with donors as well as to foster collective action in response to the challenges of Covid-19.

For instance, online donation platforms such as giving.sg and Give2Asia sought to raise funds and recruit volunteers for non-profits. Aside from providing financial assistance and food to individuals and families in need, these platforms funded efforts to provide temporary accommodation for quarantines, provide medical equipment and facilities, as well as provide for the transport needs of healthcare workers (Give2Asia, 2022). Many of these initiatives constitute micro-level urban interventions, especially in terms of providing temporary accommodations or transport services. From a broader perspective, these platforms allow for the redistribution of urban services (i.e. housing and transport) across the city, bridging gaps in the supply of and demand for these services.

Aside from urban services, donation and giving platforms also sought to foster the development of urban and technological solutions that could be applied to Singapore's Covid-19 response efforts. For instance, the Community Foundation of Singapore set up a Sayang Sayang Fund that aimed to raise additional funds for non-profits that were looking to develop innovative solutions and strategic research that could help address the impacts of COVID-19 (Community Foundation of Singapore, 2020).

Two of the causes that received support through the Sayang Sayang Fund are Recess@Home and SeniorsOK@Home, with the former providing children from disadvantaged families with access to daily meals when they were learning from home during the circuit breaker, and the latter providing food, necessities, medical supplies, and digital solutions to elderly citizens who are not able to leave their homes (Community Foundation of Singapore, 2020). Just Cause is another example of an organisation that has sought to support non-profits and funders in building sustainable digital strategies and capabilities that could help enhance programme delivery (Just Cause, 2020). As these few examples have illustrated, CSOs played a key role in Singapore's Covid-19 response efforts.

In most instances, CSOs provided for the needy and other vulnerable communities that may have inadvertently been left out of the government's social policies and support mechanisms. Given operational constraints and the natural dispersal of vulnerable communities across different neighbourhoods and districts, it is often difficult for policymakers to reach out to each and every member of these communities. Furthermore, policy initiatives at the national level tend to be much broader and are hence not able to take the micro-level needs of every individual or community into full consideration. Given their close relationships with communities and strong presence at the neighbourhood level, CSOs are therefore important policy partners and stakeholders that can enhance existing policy efforts.

Aside from CSOs, members of the public also mobilised to provide assistance to each other during the pandemic. For instance, residents of HDB apartment blocks shared masks and sanitisers with their neighbours by attaching these to the grab handles of their lifts, often through the use of cable tie, strings, and other makeshift equipment (Lee, 2020). In some instances, sanitisers were made by groups of residents using RC facilities and subsequently placed in the lifts (Oh, 2020). Through these efforts, ground-level adaptations were made to the urban environment at the neighbourhood level. While not entirely approved by the authorities, these urban modifications were not sanctioned or prohibited either, representing an urban planning grey area that allows micro-interventions that could help provide for the needs of residents within these neighbourhoods.

Conclusion

As this chapter has briefly discussed, civil society and citizen groups played a wide range of roles in supporting Singapore's pandemic response efforts. Through the efforts of CSOs and grassroots organisations, essential supplies were distributed to needy families and individuals, while community facilities became spaces for the distribution of medical supplies and vaccines. Citizen groups were also mobilised to provide for the needs of their fellow citizens at the neighbourhood level. As we have discussed in this chapter, these efforts often involved micro-level urban interventions at the community and neighbourhood levels.

It is also important to note that while many of the ground-level urban interventions that we have discussed are driven by CSOs and other non-state entities, these efforts remained very much aligned with the government's policy needs and objectives. As Wong and Wu (2021: 13–14) have noted, '[i]n Singapore, civil society is still regarded more as an actor cooperating with the state rather than a co-decision maker or partner formulating key policy responses', reflecting 'cooperative state–society relations'. It is therefore difficult to fully ascertain the extent of civil society action in Singapore's pandemic response efforts, since much of this is embedded within broader state-led pandemic response efforts.

Hence, while societal efforts are, and will become increasingly, important in enhancing the government's pandemic and crisis response efforts, these will, for the foreseeable future, remain rooted in the Singapore government's broader policy framework and plans. It is therefore with this understanding that we will turn our attention to the Singapore government's post-Covid urban plans in the next chapter.

Note

1 Statutory boards are semi-autonomous agencies that operate under the oversight of a specific ministry and serve as policy arms of the Singapore government (Lee, 1975; Woo, 2014).

6 Plans and Dreams

Rethinking the City in a Post-Covid World

As our discussions in previous chapters have shown, the Covid-19 pandemic has brought forth wide-ranging impacts on Singapore's urban landscape. From safe distancing requirements to makeshift medical facilities, Singapore's pandemic response efforts have required the adaptation and appropriation of existing urban sites, facilities, and infrastructure for healthcare purposes. As we have also discussed in Chapter 5, ground-up initiatives by civil society and citizen groups have similarly involved micro-level adaptations to the urban environs within which citizens are embedded.

While the pandemic will no doubt pass (at this time of writing, Singapore has removed almost all its Covid-19 restrictions, including the wearing of masks in most settings), the lessons learnt and the pandemic's impacts on the city may prove far more enduring. In this chapter, we will discuss the ways in which the pandemic has factored into Singapore's longer-term urban plans and, in the process, reshaped its future urban developments. These will subsequently allow us to provide the broad outlines – faint as it may be through the vagaries of time and future events yet unfolded – of the post-pandemic city.

On 17 July 2021, Singapore's Urban Redevelopment Authority (URA) launched a year-long public engagement exercise for its long-term plan review (LTPR). Previously known as concept plans, long-term plans guide Singapore's land use and development plans for the next 50 years. Beginning with the first concept plan of 1971, long-term plans are typically reviewed every ten years in order to account for evolving trends and changing demands or preferences. It is noteworthy that the LTPR had taken place during the pandemic and hence encapsulates pandemic-related land use needs such as telecommuting or 'work-from-home' (WFH) arrangements.

In the following sections, we discuss some of the Covid-related urban trends that were discussed during the LTPR and will therefore likely be incorporated into Singapore's long-term plan.

DOI: 10.4324/9781003142553-6

Shifting Work Arrangements

While the 2020 circuit break had prompted Singapore's shift to telecommuting and WFH, these arrangements would persist well into 2022 due to the large infection surges that occurred with the emergence of the Delta and Omicron variants of the coronavirus. Even as Singapore relaxed its Covid-19 restrictions in mid-2022, the Ministry of Manpower (MOM), National Trades Union Congress (NTUC), and Singapore National Employers Federation (SNEF) continued to advocate for flexible work arrangements, arguing that these arrangements foster better work–life balance and employee retention (Abdullah, 2022).

In order to encourage flexible work arrangements, the Singaporean public service decided to take the lead by allowing public officers to telecommute for up to two days a week (Abdullah, 2022). According to the government, Singapore's public service employs about 153,000 officers across its 16 ministries and more than 50 statutory boards (Department of Statistics Singapore, 2022; Government of Singapore, 2021). This means that even without accounting for the private sector, a substantial proportion of Singapore's population is expected to remain on flexible work arrangements for the long term. This will pose significant implications for Singapore's future urban planning and urban design.

In light of this long-term shift towards flexible work arrangements as well as the changes in lifestyle and commuting patterns associated with this shift, the URA's LTPR has placed a strong emphasis on mixed-use and flexible spaces (Kang, 2020). This includes incorporating more amenities and residential developments within the central business district (CBD) as well as enhancing amenities within suburban neighbourhoods. Specifically, the URA's plans to develop more public housing, or Housing and Development Board (HDB) apartment blocks in the CBD, can help prevent it from becoming a mono-use office district that may hollow out should more workers shift to WFH arrangements.

Aside from the URA's land use plans, the pandemic has also reshaped urban design in workspaces across Singapore. This includes the need to incorporate features such as better ventilation, air filtration, automatic doors, contactless fittings, hand sanitisers, and temperature-monitoring stations within office buildings (Ng, 2020). For companies that have pivoted to permanent hybrid work arrangements, office space design has increasingly prioritised amenities and collaboration spaces over desks and cubicles (Chew, 2021a).

Creating Space

The Covid-19 pandemic has also revealed the pressing need for space in the event of a pandemic. From a public health perspective, the outbreak of an airborne infectious disease will require the imposition of social distancing rules and a greater spacing out of crowds and individuals. This can be particularly challenging in highly dense and space-constrained Singapore. This means a need to create space on an ad hoc basis during an outbreak. This includes creating more space in offices and public venues through moveable furniture, as well as the ability to set up contact tracing facilities in the event of an outbreak.

As we have discussed in previous chapters, social distancing also requires more intensive management of spaces and people flows in public spaces. This includes creating single points of entry to malls and other public spaces, as well as implementing ground demarcations that regulate crowd flows into and within such spaces. The creation of space and distance within public spaces therefore involves the regulation of human flows across spaces, often through modifications to entryways and public spaces, as well as the deployment of enforcement officers for crowd control purposes.

Aside from social distancing, the pandemic has also revealed a need to cater for patient care and isolation spaces during an outbreak. Despite the presence of the National Centre for Infectious Diseases (NCID) and post-SARS efforts to expand isolation wards and facilities across Singapore's hospitals, Singapore's healthcare system nonetheless found itself strained and at risk of becoming overwhelmed during the Delta and Omicron waves of the pandemic. This was particularly the case when Singapore's vaccination levels were not high enough to provide sufficient protection.

As we have discussed in earlier chapters, the surge in infections required Singapore to convert existing spaces into makeshift isolation and treatment facilities. This includes creating community care facilities (CCFs) in the Singapore Expo exhibition halls as well as holiday chalets such as D'Resort NTUC Chalet and Village Hotel (Goei and Tiruchittampalam, 2020; Ministry of Health, 2021; Teo, 2021). In order to prevent imported cases of Covid-19, hotels were also converted into quarantine facilities for incoming travellers.

Aside from hotels and exhibition halls, Singapore has also redesigned terminal 5 of its Changi International Airport for greater 'pandemic readiness' by having smaller sub-terminals that can be converted for contingent uses, such as the testing or segregation of high-risk passengers (Mohan, 2022). These sub-terminals will also allow airport authorities to separate and isolate passengers arriving on different flights.

As we had discussed in Chapter 4, spaces such as hotels, exhibition halls, and airport terminals naturally become vacant as events and global travel are disrupted during a pandemic.

Aside from these, Singapore has also redesigned the upcoming terminal 5 of its Changi International Airport for greater pandemic resilience (Mohan, 2022). Ensuring that such spaces can easily be converted into isolation and care facilities will allow for a more efficient reallocation of people – and spatial needs – across and within the city during the outbreak of an infectious disease. By ensuring greater flexibility in the use of spaces and facilities, the city itself can be mobilised as a tool for combating pandemics during an outbreak (Woo, 2022).

Conclusion: Planning the Post-Covid City

The Covid-19 pandemic has given rise to far-ranging urban implications for cities across the world. As we have discussed in earlier chapters, Covid-19's mode of transmission – namely, airborne droplets and surface contact – made it particularly transmissible within densely populated and globally connected global cities such as Singapore. As we had alluded to, this is by no means unique to Covid-19. Previous pandemics such as the SARS outbreak had similarly spread across cities through air travel and, within them, through direct human contact.

To a greater extent than SARS, however, Covid-19 has given rise to greater urban impacts and sparked off more urban interventions in response. This is due in part to the greater severity and transmissibility of Covid-19, as well as the greater speed with which it has spread across the world. As we have discussed throughout this book, Covid-19 has given rise to far-ranging impacts on, and changes to, Singapore's urban landscape.

Even as Singapore has removed nearly all Covid-19 restrictions in its transition to 'Covid-19 resilience' (Ministry of Health, 2022c), many of the lessons that were gleaned from Covid-19 will likely continue to be encoded and embedded within Singapore's urban environs (Woo, 2022). This is particularly the case with the URA's long-term plan, which has incorporated many of the urban impacts and interventions that had arisen during the pandemic into Singapore's urban planning considerations for the next few decades.

Moving forward, urban planners and policymakers will need to ensure pandemic resilience and readiness in their city plans and urban designs. This will facilitate key pandemic response efforts such as social distancing, quarantine and isolation, patient care, and remote work. Broadly speaking, we can think of these efforts as ***regulating urban flows across space and time***.

During a pandemic, space is both a consideration and a resource that is of utmost importance. Designing for space during a pandemic will require creating more buffers and regulating the flow of people into and out of public venues and spaces. As we have discussed in Chapter 3, this involves many of the urban interventions that were implemented to facilitate social distancing. Aside from space, it is also important to consider time in pandemic-resilient urban designs. This involves creating more quarantine, isolation, and patient care facilities so as to expand healthcare capacity and buy time for policymakers to manage the multiple waves of infection.

Urban planning for a pandemic-resilient city therefore includes both spatial and temporal aspects, with effective urban designs and interventions allowing policymakers to reduce the risks of infection through social distancing and buy enough time to manage the multifaceted impacts of an outbreak through the creation of ad hoc healthcare and isolation facilities. Time and space are therefore important considerations for ensuring pandemic-resilient urban plans and designs. Even as Singapore and the rest of the world continue to exit the pandemic, it remains necessary to encode and institutionalise the lessons that were learnt from Covid-19 in our urban plans and environs.

References

Abdullah AZ (2022) Companies encouraged to have permanent flexible work arrangements, public service to take the lead. Available at: www.channelnewsasia.com/singapore/flexible-work-arrangements-work-home-covid-19-workplace-rules-eased-tripartite-guidelines-2643036 (accessed 9 September 2022).

Abouk R and Heydari B (2021) The immediate effect of COVID-19 policies on social-distancing behavior in the United States. *Public Health Reports* 136(2). SAGE Publishing: 245–252.

Adger WN (2000) Social and ecological resilience: are they related? *Progress in Human Geography* 24(3): 347–364.

Adger WN, Brown K, Nelson DR, et al. (2011) Resilience implications of policy responses to climate change. *Wiley Interdisciplinary Reviews: Climate Change* 2(5): 757–766.

Adger WN, Hughes TP, Folke C, et al. (2005) Social-ecological resilience to coastal disasters. *Science* 309(5737): 1036–1039.

Ahsan M (2020) Strategic decisions on urban built environment to pandemics in Turkey: lessons from COVID-19. *Journal of Urban Management* 9(3): 281–285.

Alfaifi A, Darraj A and El-Setouhy M (2022) The psychological impact of quarantine during the COVID-19 pandemic on quarantined non-healthcare workers, quarantined healthcare workers, and medical staff at the quarantine facility in Saudi Arabia. *Psychology Research and Behavior Management* 15: 1259–1270.

Alirol E, Getaz L, Stoll B, et al. (2011) Urbanisation and infectious diseases in a globalised world. *The Lancet Infectious Diseases* 11(2): 131–141.

Alkhamees AA, Aljohani MS, Alghesen MA, et al. (2020) Psychological distress in quarantine designated facility during COVID-19 pandemic in Saudi Arabia. *Risk Management and Healthcare Policy* 13. Dove Press: 3103–3120.

Allam Z and Jones DS (2020) Pandemic stricken cities on lockdown. Where are our planning and design professionals [now, then and into the future]? *Land Use Policy* 97: 104805.

Ang HM (2020) Former school buildings among 36 state properties to be converted to temporary housing for migrant workers. Available at: www.

channelnewsasia.com/singapore/covid-19-migrant-workers-housing-former-schools-state-properties-643696 (accessed 20 June 2022).

Ang P (2021) DBS to cut office space by 20% in next few years: CEO. *The Straits Times*, 30 April. Singapore. Available at: www.straitstimes.com/business/banking/dbs-to-cut-office-space-by-20-in-next-few-years-ceo (accessed 28 May 2022).

Ankel S (2020) A construction expert broke down how China built an emergency hospital to treat Wuhan coronavirus patients in just 10 days. Available at: www.businessinsider.com/how-china-managed-build-entirely-new-hospital-in-10-days-2020-2 (accessed 3 May 2021).

Arsenault C, Gage A, Kim MK, et al. (2022) COVID-19 and resilience of healthcare systems in ten countries. *Nature Medicine*. Nature Publishing Group: 1–11.

Baharudin H (2020) Wearable device for Covid-19 contact tracing to be rolled out soon, may be issued to everyone in Singapore. Available at: www.straitstimes.com/politics/parliament-wearable-device-for-contact-tracing-set-to-be-issued-tracetogether-does-not-work (accessed 15 June 2020).

Baker JA and Mohan M (2020) Stretched but coping: how Singapore's healthcare system has cranked up efforts to deal with COVID-19. Available at: www.channelnewsasia.com/news/singapore/covid-19-singapore-health-capacity-hospitals-treatment-12698282 (accessed 30 March 2021).

Barr MD (2014) *The Ruling Elite of Singapore: Networks of Power and Influence*. London: I.B. Tauris.

Baum SD (2015) Risk and resilience for unknown, unquantifiable, systemic, and unlikely/catastrophic threats. *Environment Systems and Decisions* 35(2): 229–236.

Bereitschaft B and Scheller D (2020) How might the COVID-19 pandemic affect 21st century urban design, planning, and development? *Urban Science* 4(4). 4. Multidisciplinary Digital Publishing Institute: 56.

Berkes F and Folke C (2003) *Navigating Social-Ecological Systems: Building Resilience for Complexity and Change*. Cambridge, UK: Cambridge University Press.

BINUH (2020) Statement by Antonio Guterres on the impact of COVID-19 in urban areas. Available at: https://binuh.unmissions.org/en/statement-antonio-guterres-impact-covid-19-urban-areas (accessed 12 January 2024).

Bloomberg News (2022) China builds more than 60 makeshift hospitals to nail Covid. *Bloomberg.com*, 22 March. Available at: www.bloomberg.com/news/articles/2022-03-22/china-to-build-more-than-60-makeshift-hospitals-to-tackle-covid (accessed 13 June 2022).

Bravata DM, Perkins AJ, Myers LJ, et al. (2021) Association of intensive care unit patient load and demand with mortality rates in US Department of Veterans Affairs hospitals during the COVID-19 pandemic. *JAMA Network Open* 4(1): e2034266.

Brunet G, Girona A, Fajardo G, et al. (2021) The contributions of civil society to food security in the context of COVID-19: a qualitative exploration in Uruguay. *Public Health Nutrition* 24(16). Cambridge University Press: 5524–5533.

Cai Q, Okada A, Jeong BG, et al. (2021) Civil society responses to the COVID-19 pandemic: a comparative study of China, Japan, and South Korea. *China Review* 21(1). The Chinese University of Hong Kong Press: 107–138.

Calder KE (2016) *Singapore: Smart City, Smart State*. Washington, DC: Brookings Institution Press.

Capano G and Woo JJ (2017) Resilience and robustness in policy design: a critical appraisal. *Policy Sciences* 1–28.

Capano G and Woo JJ (2018) Designing policy robustness: outputs and processes. *Policy and Society* 37(4). Routledge: 422–440.

Carlino G and Kerr WR (2015) Chapter 6 – agglomeration and innovation. In: Duranton G, Henderson JV and Strange WC (eds) *Handbook of Regional and Urban Economics*. Handbook of Regional and Urban Economics. Elsevier, pp. 349–404. Available at: www.sciencedirect.com/science/article/pii/B9780444595171000064 (accessed 7 February 2022).

Carlino GA, Chatterjee S and Hunt RM (2007) Urban density and the rate of invention. *Journal of Urban Economics* 61(3): 389–419.

Cavallo A and Ireland V (2014) Preparing for complex interdependent risks: a system of systems approach to building disaster resilience. *International Journal of Disaster Risk Reduction* 9: 181–193.

CDC (2020) COVID-19 and your health. Available at: www.cdc.gov/coronavirus/2019-ncov/prevent-getting-sick/social-distancing.html (accessed 9 April 2021).

Chen B, Marvin S and While A (2020a) Containing COVID-19 in China: AI and the robotic restructuring of future cities. *Dialogues in Human Geography* 10(2). SAGE Publishing: 238–241.

Chen S, Zhang Z, Yang J, et al. (2020b) Fangcang shelter hospitals: a novel concept for responding to public health emergencies. *The Lancet* 395(10232): 1305–1314.

Chew HM (2021a) IN FOCUS: thinking out of the cubicle – what lies ahead for hybrid working? Available at: www.channelnewsasia.com/singapore/office-home-future-hybrid-work-flexible-wfh-in-focus-225656 (accessed 15 September 2022).

Chew HM (2021b) Singapore opens Connect@Changi facility, allowing business visitors to meet without serving quarantine. Available at: www.channelnewsasia.com/singapore/connect-changi-facility-singapore-business-travellers-covid-19-359121 (accessed 20 June 2022).

Chew V (2009) Urban planning framework in Singapore | Infopedia. Available at: http://eresources.nlb.gov.sg/infopedia/articles/SIP_1565_2009-09-09.html (accessed 27 October 2020).

Chia ML, Him Chau DH, Lim KS, et al. (2021) Managing COVID-19 in a novel, rapidly deployable community isolation quarantine facility. *Annals of Internal Medicine* 174(2). American College of Physicians: 247–251.

Chiew CJ, Li Z and Lee VJ (2020) Reducing onward spread of COVID-19 from imported cases: quarantine and 'stay at home' measures for travellers and returning residents to Singapore. *Journal of Travel Medicine* 27(3): taaa049.

Chong C (2020a) About 1 million people have downloaded TraceTogether app, but more need to do so for it to be effective: Lawrence Wong. Available at: www.straitstimes.com/singapore/about-one-million-people-have-down loaded-the-tracetogether-app-but-more-need-to-do-so-for (accessed 8 June 2020).

Chong C (2020b) Patients who are well but still testing positive for Covid-19 to be moved to community isolation facility to preserve hospital capacity. Available at: www.straitstimes.com/singapore/patients-who-are-well-but-still-testing-positive-for-covid-19-to-be-moved-to-community (accessed 1 April 2020).

Clemente Á, Yubero E, Nicolás JF, et al. (2022) Changes in the concentration and composition of urban aerosols during the COVID-19 lockdown. *Environmental Research* 203: 111788.

CNA (2020) COVID-19: community isolation facility at Singapore Expo operational from April 10. Available at: www.channelnewsasia.com/singapore/ covid-19-community-isolation-facility-singapore-expo-operational-apr-10-763041 (accessed 14 June 2022).

CNA (2021) China builds hospital in 5 days after surge in COVID-19 cases. Available at: www.channelnewsasia.com/news/asia/covid-19-china-builds-hospital-five-days-surge-cases-13973464 (accessed 3 May 2021).

Committee on the Future Economy (2017) *Report of the Committee on the Future Economy*. February. Singapore: Government of Singapore.

Community Foundation of Singapore (2020) Sayang Sayang Fund continues to appeal for donations – Community Foundation of Singapore. Available at: www.cf.org.sg/2020/04/14/sayang-sayang-fund-continues-to-appeal-for-donations/ (accessed 7 August 2022).

Corburn J (2004) Confronting the challenges in reconnecting urban planning and public health. *American Journal of Public Health* 94(4). American Public Health Association: 541–546.

Corburn J (2007) Reconnecting with our roots: American urban planning and public health in the twenty-first century. *Urban Affairs Review* 42(5). SAGE Publishing: 688–713.

Corburn J (2013) *Healthy City Planning: From Neighbourhood to National Health Equity*. Abingdon, Oxon; New York: Routledge.

Costa DG and Peixoto JPJ (2020) COVID-19 pandemic: a review of smart cities initiatives to face new outbreaks. *IET Smart Cities* 2(2). IET Digital Library: 64–73.

da Schio N, Phillips A, Fransen K, et al. (2021) The impact of the COVID-19 pandemic on the use of and attitudes towards urban forests and green spaces: exploring the instigators of change in Belgium. *Urban Forestry & Urban Greening* 65: 127305.

Davoudi S, Brooks E and Mehmood A (2013) Evolutionary resilience and strategies for climate adaptation. *Planning Practice & Research* 28(3). Routledge: 307–322.

Dayson C and Damm C (2020) Re-making state-civil society relationships during the COVID 19 pandemic? An English perspective. *People, Place & Policy* 14(3): 282–289.

Department of Statistics Singapore (2022) Government employees. In: *The Public Service*. Available at: https://tablebuilder.singstat.gov.sg/table/TS/ M182831 (accessed 9 September 2022).

Dhillon (2021) India's hospitals overwhelmed, graveyards overflowing as virus cases surge. Available at: www.scmp.com/week-asia/health-envi ronment/article/3129532/coronavirus-india-sees-melting-crematoria-over flowing (accessed 12 June 2022).

Downey DC (2017) *Cities and Disasters*. Boca Raton, FL: CRC Press.

Duranton G and Puga D (2020) The economics of urban density. *Journal of Economic Perspectives* 34(3): 3–26.

Earl C (2020) Living with authoritarianism: Ho Chi Minh City during COVID-19 Lockdown. *City & Society* 32(2).

El Kenawy AM, Lopez-Moreno JI, McCabe MF, et al. (2021) The impact of COVID-19 lockdowns on surface urban heat island changes and air-quality improvements across 21 major cities in the Middle East. *Environmental Pollution* 288: 117802.

Eraydin A and Taşan-Kok T (2013) Introduction: resilience thinking in urban planning. In: Eraydin A and Taşan-Kok T (eds) *Resilience Thinking in Urban Planning*. Heidelberg: Springer, pp. 1–16.

Erdönmez C and Atmiş E (2021) The impact of the Covid-19 pandemic on green space use in Turkey: is closing green spaces for use a solution? *Urban Forestry & Urban Greening* 64: 127295.

Folke C, Carpenter S, Elmqvist T, et al. (2002) Resilience and sustainable development: building adaptive capacity in a world of transformations. *AMBIO: A Journal of the Human Environment* 31(5): 437–440.

Folke C, Carpenter SR, Walker B, et al. (2010) Resilience thinking: integrating resilience, adaptability and transformability. *Ecology and Society* 15(2): 20–28.

Food Bank Singapore (2020) Food pantry. Available at: https://foodbank.sg/our-big-projects/food-pantry/ (accessed 31 July 2022).

Friesen J and Pelz PF (2020) COVID-19 and slums: a pandemic highlights gaps in knowledge about urban poverty. *JMIR Public Health and Surveillance* 6(3).

Gamelas C, Abecasis L, Canha N, et al. (2021) The impact of COVID-19 confinement measures on the air quality in an urban-industrial area of Portugal. *Atmosphere* 12(9). 9. Multidisciplinary Digital Publishing Institute: 1097.

Ganapathy K (2022) New COVID-19 treatment facility for children and elderly opens at Singapore Expo. Available at: www.channelnewsasia.com/singapore/covid-19-new-treatment-facility-children-elderly-singapore-expo-moh-ong-ye-kung-2497321 (accessed 17 June 2022).

George C (2017) *Singapore, Incomplete: Reflections on a First World Nation's Arrested Political Development*. Singapore: Ethos Books. Available at: www.ethosbooks.com.sg/products/singapore-incomplete (accessed 26 June 2019).

GFP (2020) 2020 Singapore military strength. Available at: www.globalfire power.com/country-military-strength-detail.asp?country_id=singapore (accessed 19 October 2020).

Give2Asia (2022) Support local COVID-19 relief in Singapore. Available at: https://give2asia.org/covid-19-pandemic-response-singapore/ (accessed 7 August 2022).

Glaeser EL (2022) Urban resilience. *Urban Studies* 59(1). SAGE Publishing: 3–35.

Glaeser EL (2012) *Triumph of the City: How Our Greatest Invention Makes Us Richer, Smarter, Greener, Healthier, and Happier*. New York, NY: Penguin Books.

Goei A and Tiruchittampalam M (2020) Community care facility-A novel concept to deal with the COVID-19 pandemic: a Singaporean institution's experience. *Journal of Public Health Management and Practice: JPHMP* 26(6): 613–621.

Golechha M (2020) COVID-19 containment in Asia's largest urban Slum Dharavi-Mumbai, India: lessons for policymakers globally. *Journal of Urban Health: Bulletin of the New York Academy of Medicine*: 1–6.

Government Digital Services (2020) TraceTogether. Available at: www.trace together.gov.sg/ (accessed 9 April 2020).

Government of Singapore (2020) Improved standards of new dormitories for migrant workers. Available at: www.gov.sg/article/improved-standards-of-new-dormitories-for-migrant-workers (accessed 20 June 2022).

Government of Singapore (2021) The public service. Available at: www.careers. gov.sg/who-we-are/the-public-service (accessed 9 September 2022).

Greenberg MR and Schneider D (2017) *Urban Planning and Public Health*. 1st edition. Washington, DC: American Public Health Association.

Guo Y and Woo JJ (2016) *Singapore and Switzerland: Secrets to Small State Success*. Hackensack, New Jersey: World Scientific Publishing Co.

Guterres A (2020) *COVID-19 in an Urban World*. United Nations. Available at: www.un.org/en/coronavirus/covid-19-urban-world (accessed 15 October 2020).

Hall ET (1966) *The Hidden Dimension*. New York: Doubleday.

Hamidi S, Sabouri S and Ewing R (2020) Does density aggravate the COVID-19 pandemic? *Journal of the American Planning Association* 86(4). Routledge: 495–509.

Hananel R, Fishman R and Malovicki-Yaffe N (2022) Urban diversity and epidemic resilience: the case of the COVID-19. *Cities* 122: 103526.

Harpham T, Burton S and Blue I (2001) Healthy city projects in developing countries: the first evaluation. *Health Promotion International* 16(2): 111–125.

Hartley K and Jarvis DSL (2020) Policymaking in a low-trust state: legitimacy, state capacity, and responses to COVID-19 in Hong Kong. *Policy and Society* 39(3). Routledge: 403–423.

Henssler J, Stock F, van Bohemen J, et al. (2021) Mental health effects of infection containment strategies: quarantine and isolation – a systematic review and meta-analysis. *European Archives of Psychiatry and Clinical Neuroscience* 271(2): 223–234.

Her M (2020) How is COVID-19 affecting South Korea? What is our current strategy? *Disaster Medicine and Public Health Preparedness* 14(5). Cambridge University Press: 684–686.

Herman K and Drozda Ł (2021) Green infrastructure in the time of social distancing: urban policy and the tactical pandemic urbanism. *Sustainability* 13(4). 4. Multidisciplinary Digital Publishing Institute: 1632.

Ho E (2016) Smart subjects for a smart nation? Governing (smart)mentalities in Singapore. *Urban Studies*: 0042098016664305.

Hoehner CM, Brennan LK, Brownson RC, et al. (2003) Opportunities for integrating public health and urban planning approaches to promote active community environments. *American Journal of Health Promotion* 18(1). SAGE Publishing: 14–20.

Holling CS (1973) Resilience and stability of ecological systems. *Annual Review of Ecology and Systematics* 4: 1–23.

Hossain MS, Muhammad G and Guizani N (2020) Explainable AI and mass surveillance system-based healthcare framework to combat COVID-I9 like pandemics. *IEEE Network* 34(4): 126–132.

Hu M and Sidel M (2020) Civil society and COVID in China: responses in an authoritarian society. *Nonprofit and Voluntary Sector Quarterly* 49(6). SAGE Publishing: 1173–1181.

Huang Y and Li R (2022) The lockdown, mobility, and spatial health disparities in COVID-19 pandemic: a case study of New York City. *Cities* 122: 103549.

IHiS (2022) COVID 19 community care facility at expo, powered by Health-Tech. Available at: www.ihis.com.sg/Project_Showcase/covid-19/Pages/covid-community-care-facility-expo-healthtech.aspx (accessed 14 June 2022).

IMD (2020) *World Competitiveness Ranking*. Lausanne, Switzerland: IMD.

Jeong BG and Kim S-J (2021) The government and civil society collaboration against COVID-19 in South Korea: a single or multiple actor play? *Nonprofit Policy Forum* 12(1). De Gruyter: 165–187.

Joassart-Marcelli P, Wolch J and Salim Z (2011) Building the healthy city: the role of nonprofits in creating active urban parks. *Urban Geography* 32(5). Routledge: 682–711.

Johnson TF, Hordley LA, Greenwell MP, et al. (2021) Associations between COVID-19 transmission rates, park use, and landscape structure. *Science of the Total Environment* 789: 148123.

Just Cause (2020) Non-profit voices from the ground during COVID-19. Available at: www.justcauseasia.org/post/non-profit-voices-from-the-ground-during-covid-19 (accessed 7 August 2022).

Kang V (2020) URA to review plans for urban renewal in CBD. Available at: www.propertyguru.com.sg/property-management-news/2020/6/189115/covid-19-sharpens-need-for-mixed-use-developments-in-cbd (accessed 9 September 2022).

Kearney (2019) *Global Cities Index 2019*. New York, NY: Kearney. Available at: www.kearney.com/global-cities/2019 (accessed 19 October 2020).

Keil R and Ali SH (2011) The urban political pathology of emerging infectious disease in the age of the global city. In: McCann E and Ward K (eds) *Mobile Urbanism: Cities and Policymaking in the Global Age*. Minneapolis: University of Minnesota Press, pp. 123–146.

Kent JL, Harris P, Sainsbury P, et al. (2018) Influencing urban planning policy: an exploration from the perspective of public health. *Urban Policy and Research* 36(1). Routledge: 20–34.

Khan JR, Awan N, Islam MdM, et al. (2020) Healthcare capacity, health expenditure, and civil society as predictors of COVID-19 case fatalities: a global analysis. *Frontiers in Public Health* 8.

Klaus I (2020) Pandemics are also an urban planning problem. *Bloomberg.com*, 6 March. Available at: www.bloomberg.com/news/articles/2020-03-06/how-the-coronavirus-could-change-city-planning (accessed 14 December 2020).

Klein RJT, Nicholls RJ and Thomalla F (2003) Resilience to natural hazards: how useful is this concept? *Global Environmental Change Part B: Environmental Hazards* 5(1–2): 35–45.

Kok Y (2021) Larger living spaces, better ventilation among improved standards for new migrant worker dorms. *The Straits Times*, 17 September. Singapore. Available at: www.straitstimes.com/singapore/improved-standards-for-new-migrant-worker-dormitories (accessed 20 June 2022).

Kolesnikov-Jessop S (2010) Singapore exports its government expertise in urban planning (Published 2010). *The New York Times*, 27 April. Available at: www.nytimes.com/2010/04/28/business/global/28urban.html (accessed 5 November 2020).

Kong L and Woods O (2018) The ideological alignment of smart urbanism in Singapore: critical reflections on a political paradox. *Urban Studies* 55(4): 679–701.

Kövér Á (2021) The relationship between government and civil society in the era of COVID-19. *Nonprofit Policy Forum* 12(1). De Gruyter: 1–24.

Kövér Á, Antal A and Deák I (2021) Civil society and COVID-19 in Hungary: the complete annexation of civil space. *Nonprofit Policy Forum* 12(1). De Gruyter: 93–126.

Kumi E (2022) Pandemic democracy: the nexus of covid-19, shrinking civic space for civil society organizations and the 2020 elections in Ghana. *Democratization* 29(5). Routledge: 939–957.

Kummitha RKR (2020) Smart technologies for fighting pandemics: the techno- and human- driven approaches in controlling the virus transmission. *Government Information Quarterly* 37(3): 101481.

Kurohi R and Lim J (2021) Automated check-in gantries deployed at Novena's Square 2 and other malls. *The Straits Times*, 4 May. Singapore. Available at: www.straitstimes.com/singapore/consumer/automated-check-in-gantries-deployed-at-novenas-square-2-and-other-malls (accessed 6 December 2023).

Kwok CYT, Wong MS, Chan KL, et al. (2021) Spatial analysis of the impact of urban geometry and socio-demographic characteristics on COVID-19, a study in Hong Kong. *Science of The Total Environment* 764: 144455.

Lam F (2021) Singapore needs land that can be easily converted to other uses: Desmond Lee, Real Estate. *The Business Times*. Available at: www.businesstimes.com.sg/real-estate/singapore-needs-land-that-can-be-easily-converted-to-other-uses-desmond-lee (accessed 13 June 2022).

Lee BH (1975) *Statutory Boards in Singapore*. Singapore: Department of Political Science, University of Singapore.

Lee D, Heo K and Seo Y (2020) COVID-19 in South Korea: lessons for developing countries. *World Development* 135: 105057.

Lee Kuan Yew School of Public Policy (2019) Singapore's healthcare system through the years. Available at: https://lkyspp.nus.edu.sg/gia/article/singapore's-healthcare-system-through-the-years (accessed 12 December 2020).

Lee KY (2000) *From Third World to First: The Singapore Story: 1965–2000.* Singapore: Times Editions.

Lee L and Zalizan T (2022) Co-working spaces here to stay despite mass return to office, as more MNCs adopt 'hub and spoke' model post-pandemic. Available at: www.todayonline.com/singapore/hybrid-work-arrangements-mnc-co-working-spaces-1887111 (accessed 31 May 2022).

Lee M (2020) 'Proud this person is in our block': residents touched by gesture of neighbour who put masks, sanitisers in lifts. Available at: www.today online.com/singapore/proud-have-person-our-block-residents-touched-gesture-caring-neighbour-who-put-masks (accessed 31 July 2022).

Lee U-W (2021) SHN reduced to 10 days for travellers from 21 countries including US and UK. Available at: www.businesstimes.com.sg/govern ment-economy/shn-reduced-to-10-days-for-travellers-from-21-countries-including-us-and-uk (accessed 17 June 2022).

Li B, Peng Y, He H, et al. (2021) Built environment and early infection of COVID-19 in urban districts: a case study of Huangzhou. *Sustainable Cities and Society* 66: 102685.

Li T, Yuan L, Hou G, et al. (2022) Rapid design and construction management of emergency hospital during the COVID-19 epidemic. *Structural Engineering International* 32(2). Taylor & Francis: 142–146.

Lim J (2020a) 21 HDB blocks in Redhill Close to house healthy essential foreign workers relocated from dorms. Available at: www.todayonline.com/singapore/some-healthy-foreign-workers-essential-services-moved-their-dormitories-redhill-close (accessed 20 June 2022).

Lim J (2020b) Migrant workers move out of temporary housing in Bukit Merah, return to dorms. *The Straits Times*, 30 December. Singapore. Available at: www.straitstimes.com/singapore/jobs/migrant-workers-move-out-of-tempo rary-housing-in-bukit-merah-return-to-dorms (accessed 20 June 2022).

Lim J (2021) More firms in Singapore set to cut office space in coming months amid Covid-19. *The Straits Times*, 4 July. Singapore. Available at: www. straitstimes.com/business/property/more-singapore-firms-set-to-cut-office-space-in-coming-months-amid-covid-19 (accessed 28 May 2022).

Lim LYC (2015) Fifty years of development in the Singapore economy: an introductory review. *The Singapore Economic Review* 60(03): 1502002.

Lopez B, Kennedy C, Field C, et al. (2021) Who benefits from urban green spaces during times of crisis? Perception and use of urban green spaces in New York City during the COVID-19 pandemic. *Urban Forestry & Urban Greening* 65: 127354.

Low L (2006) *The Political Economy of a City-State Revised.* Singapore: Marshall Cavendish.

Low Y (2022) New Covid-19 treatment facility set up at Singapore Expo, with 600 beds for children and caregivers. *TODAY*, 14 February. Available at: www.todayonline.com/singapore/new-covid-19-treatment-facility-set-singapore-expo-600-beds-children-and-caregivers-1816361 (accessed 13 January 2024).

Malone-Lee LC (2019) What the 2019 master plan says about Singapore's approach to land use. Available at: www.todayonline.com/commentary/what-2019-master-plan-says-about-singapores-approach-land-use (accessed 3 November 2020).

Marinelli M (2020) Emergency healthcare facilities: managing design in a post Covid-19 world. *IEEE Engineering Management Review* 48(4): 65–71.

Matrajt L and Leung T (2020) Evaluating the effectiveness of social distancing interventions to delay or flatten the epidemic curve of coronavirus disease. *Emerging Infectious Diseases* 26(8): 1740–1748.

Matthew RA and McDonald B (2006) Cities under Siege: urban planning and the threat of infectious disease. *Journal of the American Planning Association* 72(1). Routledge: 109–117.

Mayen Huerta C and Utomo A (2021) Evaluating the association between urban green spaces and subjective well-being in Mexico City during the COVID-19 pandemic. *Health & Place* 70: 102606.

McClory J (2019) *The Soft Power 30*. California, USA: USC Center on Public Diplomacy.

Mehmood A (2016) Of resilient places: planning for urban resilience. *European Planning Studies* 24(2). Routledge: 407–419.

Mehta V (2020) The new proxemics: COVID-19, social distancing, and sociable space. *Journal of Urban Design* 25(6). Routledge: 669–674.

Mera AP and Balijepalli C (2020) Towards improving resilience of cities: an optimisation approach to minimising vulnerability to disruption due to natural disasters under budgetary constraints. *Transportation* 47(4): 1809–1842.

Miao Q, Schwarz S and Schwarz G (2021) Responding to COVID-19: community volunteerism and coproduction in China. *World Development* 137: 105128.

Milne GJ and Xie S (2020) The effectiveness of social distancing in mitigating COVID-19 spread: a modelling analysis. *medRxiv*. Available at: www.medrxiv.org/content/10.1101/2020.03.20.20040055v1 (accessed 25 January 2022).

Ministry of Finance (2020) More support for workers and jobs through the jobs support scheme and COVID-19 support grant. Available at: www.gov. sg/article/more-support-for-workers-and-jobs-through-the-jobs-support-scheme-and-covid-19-support-grant (accessed 13 October 2020).

Ministry of Finance (2022) Emerging stronger as one. Available at: www.mof. gov.sg/singapore-public-sector-outcomes-review/citizens/safeguarding-our-way-of-life/emerging-stronger-as-one (accessed 28 July 2022).

Ministry of Health (2020a) Additional precautionary measures to prevent further importation and spread of Covid-19 cases. Available at: www.moh. gov.sg/news-highlights/details/additional-precautionary-measures-to-pre vent-further-importation-and-spread-of-covid-19-cases (accessed 18 May 2020).

Ministry of Health (2020b) Expansion of the enhanced stay-home notice requirements to all countries. Available at: www.moh.gov.sg/news-high lights/details/expansion-of-the-enhanced-stay-home-notice-requirements-to-all-countries (accessed 17 June 2022).

Ministry of Health (2020c) Measures to contain the Covid-19 outbreak in migrant worker dormitories. Available at: www.moh.gov.sg/news-high lights/details/measures-to-contain-the-covid-19-outbreak-in-migrant-worker-dormitories (accessed 16 June 2022).

Ministry of Health (2020d) Stricter safe distancing measures to prevent further spread of Covid-19 cases. Available at: www.moh.gov.sg/news-highlights/details/stricter-safe-distancing-measures-to-prevent-further-spread-of-covid-19-cases (accessed 18 May 2020).

Ministry of Health (2021) Setting up of stepped-up community care facilities. Available at: www.moh.gov.sg/news-highlights/details/setting-up-of-stepped-up-community-care-facilities.

Ministry of Health (2022a) Covid-19 statistics. Available at: https://data.gov.sg/dataset/covid-19-case-numbers/resource/aa6ba85e-c256-4eef-99ca-7849c7d6f148/view/17121d71-f005–4a96–8b74-cf9e7bee8121 (accessed 1 June 2022).

Ministry of Health (2022b) Target criteria before Covid-19 restrictions are lifted and normal dining and socialising allowed. Available at: www.moh.gov.sg/news-highlights/details/target-criteria-before-covid-19-restrictions-are-lifted-and-normal-dining-and-socialising-allowed (accessed 1 June 2022).

Ministry of Health (2022c) Transition phase to Covid-19 resilience. Available at: www.moh.gov.sg/covid-19-phase-advisory (accessed 8 June 2022).

Ministry of Manpower Singapore (n.d.) Updated advisory on COVID-19 vaccination at the workplace. Available at: www.mom.gov.sg/workplace-safety-and-health/workplace-resilience-against-infectious-diseases/advisory-on-covid-19-vaccination-in-employment-settings (accessed 6 December 2023).

Mohan M (2022) NDR 2022: Changi Airport's terminal 5 project redesigned to be pandemic-ready, more energy-efficient. Available at: www.channelnewsasia.com/singapore/changi-airport-t5-redesigned-pandemic-ready-ndr2022-pm-lee-2891301 (accessed 10 September 2022).

Moosa IA (2020) The effectiveness of social distancing in containing Covid-19. *Applied Economics* 52(58). Routledge: 6292–6305.

The Mori Memorial Foundation (2019) Global Power City Index 2019. Available at: www.mori-m-foundation.or.jp/english/ius2/gpci2/2019.shtml (accessed 19 October 2020).

Mouratidis K (2021) How COVID-19 reshaped quality of life in cities: a synthesis and implications for urban planning. *Land Use Policy* 111: 105772.

National Library Board (2014) First master plan is approved – Singapore history. Available at: https://eresources.nlb.gov.sg/history/events/ef5af33f-bc66-4080-81d4-013564ba3119 (accessed 3 November 2020).

Neiderud C-J (2015) How urbanization affects the epidemiology of emerging infectious diseases. *Infection Ecology & Epidemiology* 5(1). Taylor & Francis: 27060.

Ng JS (2020) URA reviewing urban plans for CBD, heartlands as Covid-19 'sharpens need' for changing amenities in districts. Available at: www.todayonline.com/singapore/ura-reviewing-urban-plans-cbd-heartlands-covid-19-sharpens-need-changing-amenities-districts (accessed 10 September 2022).

Norris FH, Stevens SP, Pfefferbaum B, et al. (2007) Community resilience as a metaphor, theory, set of capacities, and strategy for disaster readiness. *American Journal of Community Psychology* 41(1–2): 127–150.

OECD (2020) *Cities Policy Responses. OECD Policy Responses to Coronavirus (Covid-19)*, 23 July. Paris, France: OECD. Available at: www.oecd.org/coronavirus/policy-responses/cities-policy-responses-fd1053ff/ (accessed 1 May 2021).

Oh T (2020) Heroes unmasked: no hand sanitiser? No fear. These 'super mums' are here to help. Available at: www.todayonline.com/singapore/heroes-unmasked-no-hand-sanitiser-no-fear-these-super-mums-are-here-help (accessed 31 July 2022).

Olds K and Yeung H (2004) Pathways to global city formation: a view from the developmental city-state of Singapore. *Review of International Political Economy* 11(3): 489–521.

Ortmann S (2011) Singapore: authoritarian but newly competitive. *Journal of Democracy* 22(4): 153–164.

Panda A (2020) Singapore: a small Asian heavyweight. Available at: www.cfr.org/backgrounder/singapore-small-asian-heavyweight (accessed 19 October 2020).

Pelling M (2012) *The Vulnerability of Cities: Natural Disasters and Social Resilience*. London, U.K.: Routledge.

People's Association (2015) About us. Available at: www.pa.gov.sg/About_Us (accessed 28 June 2016).

Petersen A (1996) The 'healthy' city, expertise, and the regulation of space. *Health & Place* 2(3): 157–165.

Phua R and Ang HM (2020) 'Dedicated strategy' to break COVID-19 spread in dormitories, including housing healthy workers in army camps. Available at: www.channelnewsasia.com/news/singapore/covid-19-foreign-worker-dormitories-range-of-measures-12625624 (accessed 6 May 2020).

Qian M and Jiang J (2020) COVID-19 and social distancing. *Journal of Public Health*: 1–3.

Rajaratnam S (1972) *Singapore: Global City*. Singapore Press Club. Available at: www.nas.gov.sg/archivesonline/data/pdfdoc/PressR19720206a.pdf.

Ramchandani N (2020) Hotels roll with the punches to keep rooms occupied. Available at: www.businesstimes.com.sg/government-economy/hotels-roll-with-the-punches-to-keep-rooms-occupied (accessed 17 June 2022).

Rodan G (2008) Singapore "Exceptionalism"? authoritarian rule and state transformation. In: Wong J and Friedman E (eds) *Political Transitions in Dominant Party Systems: Learning to Lose*. New York: Routledge, pp. 231–251.

Rozario PA and Rosetti AL (2012) 'Many helping hands': a review and analysis of long-term care policies, programs, and practices in Singapore. *Journal of Gerontological Social Work* 55(7): 641–658.

Sacchetto D, Raviolo M, Beltrando C, et al. (2020) COVID-19 surge capacity solutions: our experience of converting a concert hall into a temporary hospital for mild and moderate COVID-19 patients. *Disaster Medicine and Public Health Preparedness*. Cambridge University Press: 1–4.

Sanderson D (2000) Cities, disasters and livelihoods. *Risk Management* 2(4): 49–58.

Sarkar C, Webster C and Gallacher J (2014) *Healthy Cities: Public Health through Urban Planning*. Cheltenham, UK: Edward Elgar Publishing.

Sassen S (1999) Global Financial Centers. *Foreign Affairs* 78: 75–87.
Sassen S (2001) *Global Networks, Linked Cities*. New York, NY: Routledge.
Sassen S (2011) *Cities in a World Economy*. 4th edition. Thousand Oaks, CA: SAGE Publishing.
Sharifi A and Khavarian-Garmsir AR (2020) The COVID-19 pandemic: impacts on cities and major lessons for urban planning, design, and management. *Science of The Total Environment* 749: 142391.
Shorfuzzaman M, Hossain MS and Alhamid MF (2021) Towards the sustainable development of smart cities through mass video surveillance: a response to the COVID-19 pandemic. *Sustainable Cities and Society* 64: 102582.
Sim D and Kok X (2020) How did migrant worker dorms become Singapore's biggest Covid-19 cluster? Available at: www.scmp.com/week-asia/explained/article/3080466/how-did-migrant-worker-dormitories-become-singapores-biggest (accessed 22 May 2020).
Singh B (2017) *Understanding Singapore Politics*. 1st edition. Hackensack, New Jersey: World Scientific Publishing Co.
Soon C and Koh G (eds) (2017) *Civil Society and The State in Singapore*. London: World Scientific Europe Ltd.
Stewart GT, Kolluru R and Smith M (2009) Leveraging public-private partnerships to improve community resilience in times of disaster. *International Journal of Physical Distribution & Logistics Management* 39(5): 343–364.
The Straits Times (2020) Forum: Covid-19 or not, buildings must comply with fire safety requirements. 20 August. Singapore. Available at: www.straitstimes.com/forum/forum-covid-19-or-not-buildings-must-comply-with-fire-safety-requirements (accessed 6 December 2023).
The Straits Times (2022) Standard Chartered reduces its Singapore office space by half. Available at: www.straitstimes.com/business/banking/standard-chartered-slashes-its-singapore-office-space-by-half (accessed 28 May 2022).
Summers DJ, Cheng DH-Y, Lin PH-H, et al. (2020) Potential lessons from the Taiwan and New Zealand health responses to the COVID-19 pandemic. *The Lancet Regional Health – Western Pacific* 4: 100044.
Tai J (2016) All hands on deck needed for social good. Available at: www.straitstimes.com/opinion/all-hands-on-deck-needed-for-social-good (accessed 27 October 2020).
Tan C (2020) Some malls that lock doors to comply with Covid-19 measures are breaching fire safety rules. *The Straits Times*, 7 September. Singapore. Available at: www.straitstimes.com/singapore/some-malls-struggling-to-comply-with-fire-safety-rules-as-they-implement-covid-19-measures (accessed 6 December 2023).
Tan KP (2008) Meritocracy and elitism in a global city: ideological shifts in Singapore. *International Political Science Review/Revue internationale de science politique* 29(1): 7–27.
Tan KP (2012) The ideology of pragmatism: neo-liberal globalisation and political authoritarianism in Singapore. *Journal of Contemporary Asia* 42(1): 67–92.
Tan T (2021) *Crisis Accomodations*. Urban Solutions, June. Singapore: Centre for Livable Cities.

Tang SK (2020) Singapore in technical recession after GDP shrinks 41.2% in Q2 from preceding quarter due to COVID-19. Available at: www.channel newsasia.com/news/business/gdp-singapore-technical-recession-contrac tion-q2-mti-12927168 (accessed 16 July 2020).

Tay TF and Zhang LM (2020) Mask distribution to begin at 200 RC centres today. *The Straits Times*, 1 February. Singapore. Available at: www.strait-stimes.com/singapore/mask-distribution-to-begin-at-200-rc-centres-today (accessed 28 July 2022).

Taylor PJ (2000) World cities and territorial states under conditions of contemporary globalization. *Political Geography* 19(1): 5–32.

Tee Z (2020) Coronavirus: mega Covid-19 facility being built at Tanjong Pagar terminal to house up to 15,000 people. *The Straits Times*, 23 April. Singapore. Available at: www.straitstimes.com/singapore/health/coronavi-rus-mega-covid-19-facility-being-built-at-tanjong-pagar-terminal-to-house (accessed 22 January 2024).

Teo J (2021) Village Hotel Sentosa becomes 6th Covid-19 community care facility. *The Straits Times*, 29 July. Singapore. Available at: www.strait stimes.com/singapore/health/moh-adds-village-hotel-sentosa-to-list-of-covid-19-community-care-facilities (accessed 17 June 2022).

Teufel B, Sushama L, Poitras V, et al. (2021) Impact of COVID-19-related traffic slowdown on urban heat characteristics. *Atmosphere* 12(2). 2. Multidisciplinary Digital Publishing Institute: 243.

Toh TW (2021) Connect@Changi converted into Covid-19 community care facility. *The Straits Times*, 26 August. Singapore. Available at: www.straits times.com/singapore/transport/connectchangi-converted-into-covid-19-community-care-facility (accessed 17 June 2022).

UN-Habitat (2020) UN-Habitat report on cities and pandemics. Available at: https://unhabitat.org/un-habitat-report-on-cities-and-pandemics-towards-a-more-just-green-and-healthy-future (accessed 11 December 2020).

Urban Redevelopment Authority (2016) Our planning process. Available at: www.ura.gov.sg/uol/concept-plan/our-planning-process/our-planning-pro-cess.aspx (accessed 16 April 2017).

Urban Redevelopment Authority (2020a) Concept Plan 2011 and MND Land Use Plan. Available at: www.ura.gov.sg/Corporate/Planning/Concept-Plan/Land-Use-Plan (accessed 2 November 2020).

Urban Redevelopment Authority (2020b) Master plan. Available at: www.ura.gov.sg/Corporate/Planning/Master-Plan/Introduction (accessed 3 November 2020).

Urban Redevelopment Authority (2020c) Past concept plans. Available at: www.ura.gov.sg/Corporate/Planning/Concept-Plan/Past-Concept-Plans (accessed 31 October 2020).

Urban Redevelopment Authority (2022) What you have shared with us in phase 1. Available at: www.ura.gov.sg/Corporate/Planning/Long-Term-Plans/Long-Term-Plan-Review/Phase-1 (accessed 25 January 2022).

Valdenebro J-V, Gimena FN and López JJ (2021) The transformation of a trade fair and exhibition centre into a field hospital for COVID-19 patients via multi-utility tunnels. *Tunnelling and Underground Space Technology* 113: 103951.

Vale LJ (2014) The politics of resilient cities: whose resilience and whose city? *Building Research & Information* 42(2). Routledge: 191–201.

Wan K-M, Ka-ki Ho L, Wong NWM, et al. (2020) Fighting COVID-19 in Hong Kong: the effects of community and social mobilization. *World Development* 134: 105055.

Wang CJ, Ng CY and Brook RH (2020) Response to COVID-19 in Taiwan: big data analytics, new technology, and proactive testing. *JAMA* 323(14): 1341–1342.

Wardle M, Morris H and Mainelli M (2020) *The Global Financial Centres Index 27*. March. London: Long Finance.

WHO (2023) Singapore: WHO COVID-19 dashboard. Available at: https://covid19.who.int (accessed 29 November 2023).

Wibawa (2020) Timelapse video shows how China built a 1,000-bed hospital in 10 days. *ABC News*, 2 February. Available at: www.abc.net.au/news/2020-02-03/china-completes-wuhan-makeshift-hospital-to-treat-coronavirus/11923000 (accessed 13 June 2022).

Wong W and Wu AM (2021) *State or Civil Society – What Matters in Fighting COVID-19? A Comparative Analysis of Hong Kong and Singapore*. ID 3923618, SSRN Scholarly Paper, 14 September. Rochester, NY: Social Science Research Network. Available at: https://papers.ssrn.com/abstract=3923618 (accessed 8 December 2021).

Woo JJ (2014) Singapore's policy style: statutory boards as policymaking units. *Journal of Asian Public Policy* 8(2): 120–133.

Woo JJ (2015a) Beyond the neoliberal orthodoxy: alternative financial policy regimes in Asia's financial centres. *Critical Policy Studies* 9(3): 297–316.

Woo JJ (2015b) Policy relations and policy subsystems: financial policy in Hong Kong and Singapore. *International Journal of Public Administration* 38(8): 553–561.

Woo JJ (2016) *Business and Politics in Asia's Key Financial Centres – Hong Kong, Singapore and Shanghai*. 1st ed. Singapore: Springer.

Woo JJ (2018) *The Evolution of the Asian Developmental State: Hong Kong and Singapore*. London: Routledge.

Woo JJ (2019) The politics of policymaking: policy co-creation in Singapore's financial sector. *Policy Studies* 0(0). Routledge: 1–18.

Woo JJ (2020a) *Capacity-Building and Pandemics: Singapore's Response to Covid-19*. London: Palgrave Macmillan.

Woo JJ (2020b) Pandemic, politics and pandemonium: political capacity and Singapore's response to the Covid-19 crisis. *Policy Design and Practice* 0(0). Routledge: 1–17.

Woo JJ (2020c) Policy capacity and Singapore's response to the COVID-19 pandemic. *Policy and Society* 39(3). Routledge: 1–18.

Woo JJ (2022) The road to better pandemic planning. *The Straits Times*, 8 September. Singapore. Available at: www.straitstimes.com/opinion/the-road-to-better-pandemic-planning (accessed 10 September 2022).

World Health Organisation (2021) COVID-19 advice – physical distancing. Available at: www.who.int/westernpacific/emergencies/covid-19/information/physical-distancing (accessed 9 April 2021).

Xie J, Luo S, Furuya K, et al. (2020) Urban parks as green buffers during the COVID-19 pandemic. *Sustainability* 12(17). 17. Multidisciplinary Digital Publishing Institute: 6751.

Xu H (2020) Urban development and future cities: towards building back a better post COVID-19 Kuwait. Available at: www.undp.org/content/undp/en/home/news-centre/speeches/2020/urban-development-and-future-cities-.html (accessed 16 October 2020).

Yamazaki T, Iida A, Hino K, et al. (2021) Use of urban green spaces in the context of lifestyle changes during the COVID-19 pandemic in Tokyo. *Sustainability* 13(17). 17. Multidisciplinary Digital Publishing Institute: 9817.

Yeung HW and Olds K (1998) Singapore's global reach: situating the city-state in the global economy. *International Journal of Urban Sciences* 2(1): 24–47.

Yigitcanlar T, Butler L, Windle E, et al. (2020) Can building "artificially intelligent cities" safeguard humanity from natural disasters, pandemics, and other catastrophes? An urban scholar's perspective. *Sensors* 20(10). 10. Multidisciplinary Digital Publishing Institute: 2988.

Yong C (2022) Isolation period will remain at 7 days as some Omicron cases still presenting later. *The Straits Times*, 21 January. Singapore. Available at: www.straitstimes.com/singapore/isolation-period-will-remain-at-7-days-for-now-as-some-omicron-cases-still-presenting-later (accessed 17 June 2022).

Yong N (2021) S'pore can raise ICU capacity, 'not enough' staff: Puthucheary. Available at: https://sg.news.yahoo.com/singapore-ramp-up-icu-capacity-not-enough-people-janil-puthucheary-061622932.html (accessed 1 June 2022).

Yuen B (2009) Guiding spatial changes: Singapore urban planning. In: Lall SV, Freire M, Yuen B, et al. (eds) *Urban Land Markets: Improving Land Management for Successful Urbanization*. London: Springer, pp. 363–384.

Index

For Product Safety Concerns and Information please contact our EU
representative GPSR@taylorandfrancis.com
Taylor & Francis Verlag GmbH, Kaufingerstraße 24, 80331 München, Germany

www.ingramcontent.com/pod-product-compliance
Ingram Content Group UK Ltd.
Pitfield, Milton Keynes, MK11 3LW, UK
UKHW021112180425
457613UK00005B/56